Dear Mom —

You are more than the roots of success, you are also the flower.

Love,
Francis

The Roots of Success

The Roots of Success

Cynthia Pincus, Ph.D.
Leslie Elliott
Trudy Schlachter

Prentice-Hall, Inc., Englewood Cliffs, New Jersey

The Roots of Success by Cynthia Pincus, Ph.D., Leslie Elliott, and Trudy Schlachter
Copyright © 1980 by Cynthia Pincus, Leslie Elliott, Trudy Schlachter
Portions of this book first appeared in *Family Circle* magazine. Copyright © 1978 by Leslie Elliott and Trudy Schlachter.
All rights reserved. No part of this book may be reproduced in any form or by any means, except for the inclusion of brief quotations in a review, without permission in writing from the publisher. Address inquiries to Prentice-Hall, Inc., Englewood Cliffs, N.J. 07632
Printed in the United States of America
Prentice-Hall International, Inc., London/Prentice-Hall of Australia, Pty. Ltd., Sydney/Prentice-Hall of Canada, Ltd., Toronto/Prentice-Hall of India Private Ltd., New Delhi/Prentice-Hall of Japan, Inc., Tokyo/Prentice-Hall of Southeast Asia Pte. Ltd., Singapore/Whitehall Books Limited, Wellington, New Zealand
10 9 8 7 6 5 4 3 2 1

Library of Congress Cataloging in Publication Data
Pincus, Cynthia Sterling.
   The roots of success.
   Includes bibliographical references and index.
   1. Parenting. 2. Children—Management.
3. Mothers—Psychology. 4. Mother and child.
5. Achievement motivation in children. 6. Success.
I. Elliott, Leslie, joint author. II. Schlachter,
Trudy, joint author. III. Title.
HQ755.8.P56   649'.1   80-18462
ISBN 0-13-783258-3

For the mothers who so generously shared their insights into how they raised successful children, and for the parents of today who love and care enough to seek the same pathways.

Contents

1. The Study to Find Out What Worked   1

2. The Earth for the Roots: The Achievers' Backgrounds   14

3. Gifted Mothering: The Threefold Commitment   30

4. Gifted Mothering and the Hot Coal Technique   50

5. Mothers and Fathers: Sharing the Commitment and the Parenting Partnership   62

6. The Family Life That Fosters Achievement   79

7. Raising Children for Self-Reliance: A Key to Achievement   105

8. Inspirations for Achievement: Role Models, Mentors, and the Dream   122

9. Education Is a Full-Time Adventure   132

10. Bringing Up Achievers in Single-Parent and Working-Mother Households   151

11. Are You Raising an Achiever? Test Yourself   160

12. The Twelve Signposts for Success   171

Appendixes
    1. The Survey Questionnaire   185
    2. Sources   197

Index   203

Acknowledgments

From the beginning, nearly everyone we approached about this project was enthusiastic and generous about helping it along. We are grateful to them all, because the book could not have been done without them. Our first and biggest debt is to the mothers who responded to our survey, and to several of their achieving offspring who gave us reminiscences and insights into the experience.

The list continues with Drs. Paul Chance and Carin Rubenstein, who worked on the original *Family Circle* study on which the book is based: Dr. Chance analyzed and wrote up the data, and Dr. Rubenstein did extensive research and also reviewed this manuscript for us. Shlomo Ariel did additional research for the book. Phyllis Cohen, PhD, Yale University School of Medicine; Stephen L. Dworkin, MA, Southern Connecticut State College; Howard Gardner, PhD, Harvard University; Marianne Mossbach, MA, New York City; Judith Pasamanick, MA, Bank Street College of Education; and Gloria F. Wolinsky, PhD, Hunter College, have all contributed valuable input.

We also owe special thanks to Myrna Blyth, Connie Leisure, Paul Marshall, Dr. Willard Gaylin, Dr. Harold Marcus, Ellen Berman, Patricia Burke, Linda Cioffeletti, Jeanne Diao Cohen, Janet Adelberg Davis, Ellis Deull, Arlene Gersh, Henry and Carol Grossman, Stan Hoffman, Al Kildow, Angela Miller, Gus Morelli, Susan Morrow, Sydney Perry, Judith Schwartz, and Jerry Tokofsky, who all made special efforts in our behalf.

Finally, we acknowledge those near and dear to us for their encouragement during this long process: Jonathan, Adam, Daniel, and Jeremy Pincus; Emma and Nigel Elliott and D. J. Wells; Marvin, Brad, Scott and Kris Schlachter.

Cynthia Pincus, Leslie Elliott, Trudy Schlachter

1. The study to find out what worked

We all dream of success and satisfaction for our children. When they are tiny babies, we hold them in our arms, yet see them as the great men and women of the future. In America, the climb up the ladder is such a common phenomenon that it is almost assumed each generation will outdo the one before it. A father's hopes are not that his son will follow in his footsteps, but that he should pass far beyond in education, accomplishment, and material comfort. But are there things parents can do to help make this happen? We think there are, and that is what this book is about.

What do we mean by "successful child rearing" and "successful children"?

Though being a parent is a joy in itself, raising a child who matures into an independent, contributing adult is the classic vindication for the sacrifices of parenthood. In an era where opportunity is greater than ever before, in a society where success and stardom are exceptionally rewarded, there's an even greater pressure to raise achievers.

A child who grows up to be a winner must have ability and talent, as shown by many studies of gifted children and adult achievers. We are not suggesting that *any* youngster can be pummeled or prodded into becoming president of IBM or the conductor of the Philharmonic. Instead, we believe the secret to successful child rearing—or raising a child who matures to feel that he is, and is regarded by others, as successful—is to bring up the child to realize his or her fullest potential. Such a person is more likely to feel secure and confident, and in turn raise his or her own children successfully. This may mean something as simple as acknowledging that while *your* dream for your youngster may be the presidency of a corporation, *his* gift might be for being first or even second trombonist in a brass band! A realization of potential is really what we mean by "successful children."

Many sources contributed to the material in the book, but the inspiration and primary source was a study two of us did with Dr. Paul Chance for *Family Circle* magazine. It appeared in the April 1978 issue under the title, "The Roots of Success." This book is based heavily on its findings; additional interviews, anecdotes, and research have expanded it to its present format.

For many years social scientists have been trying to unravel the mysteries of human motivation and accomplishment—why some people succeed, while others who seem to have equivalent or even greater gifts do not. There have been hundreds of studies done on this, covering both children and adults, in schools, clinics, and laboratories. We went instead to a group of women who had actually raised children who grew up to succeed: the mothers of some of America's outstanding achievers.

We wanted to get firsthand impressions from these

women, to see if, by any chance, they showed common child-rearing attitudes and practices. Could it be that they were doing something that worked, something that could be shared with others? Were they doing something "right"?

It turned out that, indeed, despite disparities of social, economic, and financial background, size of family, and so on, these mothers did share some basic approaches to mothering and to nourishing "the roots of success" in their own children. Their children, of course, also varied—from short to tall, moody to outgoing, musical to mathematical. Some showed great promise, and others didn't display anything unusual when they were young.

Several hundred questionnaires were sent out, resulting in a final selection of 60 mothers of achievers. In making the choices, we were looking for achievers who were acknowledged for accomplishment in their own fields. Some household-word celebrities were easy, but we knew that while many achievers are celebrities, it doesn't work the other way: Many celebrities aren't achievers and a great many achievers aren't known to the public at all. There's no doubt that being recognized for achievement counts, however. Success implies not just doing something well, but having other people—whether it's a handful of colleagues in one's own specialty or millions of TV viewers—noticing and acknowledging that you do it well.

We spoke to experts, culled names from other merit lists, and used our own resources to come up with the achievers we selected. We divided them into four broad career areas. (We got a small sampling of achievers in sports, but not enough to make a separate category.) The group included such people as:

Entertainment/performing arts: Actress Faye Dunaway; comedian Chevy Chase; singer Dionne Warwick; choreographer Twyla Tharp; ballerinas Patricia McBride, Suzanne Farrell, and Judith Jamison; composer/performers Burt Bacharach and Paul Simon.

Business/politics: Corporate chairmen John H. Filer (Aetna Casualty), Edward M. Ney (Young & Rubicam), William F. May (American Can), Health and Human Services (HHS) Secretary Patricia Roberts Harris, Senator Daniel Moynihan and Congresswomen Patricia Scott Schroeder and Elizabeth Holtzman, mayors Kenneth Gibson of Newark and Maynard Jackson of Atlanta.

Science/scholarship: Nobel-prizewinning medical physicist Rosalyn Yalow; economist Eli Ginzberg; Wellesley president Barbara Newell; theologian Alfred Gottschalk; psychobiologist Sarah Fryer Leibowitz from Rockefeller University; Floyd Bloom of the Salk Institute; Daniel Callahan of The Hastings Center (Institute of Society, Ethics, and the Life Sciences in Hastings-on-Hudson, New York).

Arts/letters: Novelists Michael Crichton, John Updike; journalists Frances FitzGerald and George Plimpton; painters Jamie Wyeth, John Clem Clarke, and Larry Bell.

An exceptional group of people. They cross a very broad spectrum of achievement, and their mothers also varied widely—in age as well as ethnic, geographical, and educational backgrounds. Some of these women are extraordinary people, highly accomplished personally or professionally in their own rights. Others made equally vital contributions in less visible ways. In such a remarkable and diverse group, there are women all of us can recognize and identify with.

What about father?

Some of the survey mothers chastised us for seeming to overlook Dad. One said, "I do object that you left the father out in your survey. I haven't the slightest doubt that [my husband] ... was the greatest influence in his son's life."

It's true that in preparing the survey for *Family Circle* we did focus on Mom at the expense of Dad, for two reasons. First, because we had to keep the size of the project within limits; and second, because the bulk of available research on parental influences deals with the mother, and we wanted to compare our survey results with those from other studies.

It is certainly true that most of the survey children, like others of past generations, grew up in households where both parents were present. We have now given this relationship more attention, describing the influence of fathers and how successful parenting partnerships worked in creating a harmonious home, which turned out to be a definite factor in raising achievers.

At the same time, we are aware that today's circumstances are quite different: There are vastly more single-parent homes than there were when the survey children were being raised. This has not only established a more sympathetic environment for fatherless and motherless homes; it has also redoubled the emphasis on mother, or the mothering role of the primary parent, in creating a stable and secure base for the growing child.

Why are projects like this important?

Children are our most precious resource, and yet we know so little about them! Many educators and mental health professionals feel that children's needs are badly neglected in current research and problem solving in American culture. They recognize an urgent necessity for more information on how our fast-moving society is affecting the lives of our children, and some even advocate a national commission for this at the highest levels of government. Questions about the unknown dangers of every technology—from nuclear radiation to violence on television—often center on potential damage to children, as do those of social legislation dealing with such issues as pornography or the driving, voting, and drinking ages. The UN proclaimed 1979 as the International Year of the Child; to many, this sort of attention was long overdue.

This is not to say that research hasn't been done. It has—endlessly. But it has focused on what's wrong, on picking apart the problem once it's *become* a problem, to find out where we went off the track. For instance, we now know (because research has taught us) that abuse in early childhood is virtually a universal experience among hardcore juvenile delinquents and prison inmates from all socioeconomic backgrounds. This doesn't mean that everyone who was abused as a youngster winds up in jail; but it does suggest that since most serious offenders have this in their histories, it's a potent destructive influence.

Organizations have grown up to cope with this and similar well-documented problems. Our study is aimed at another, less obvious problem: the widespread neglect of children—a problem far harder to pin down, much less treat. It is more a sin of omission than commission—of something not done rather than something done which shouldn't have been.

Parental neglect can range from the obvious failure to provide adequate food and clothing to the less visible but equally damaging *failure to provide adequate love, care, and attention.* This is the kind of innocent, invisible neglect possible in affluent homes where necessities may be amply—even opulently—provided, but both parents are away all day at employment or leisure; houses are isolated so even neighbors can't fill the void as they might on denser urban streets.

There are no formal organizations to identify and prevent this sort of problem. We must rely on ourselves to become aware of these situations, and use our common sense and abilities to deal with them. That is why information on what works with children is even more helpful to us than finding out what failed after the fact.

Roles parents play

The "Roots" study also yielded overdue recognition for the constructive roles parents play. For years social science zeroed in on everything a parent could do wrong—from general issues such as delinquency and drug abuse to specific family miseries handled in clinics and private therapy. It has, therefore, always been easy to point to conditions in a child's home life as the source of his problem.

We have rarely tried to determine precisely the constructive approaches that enable people to rear children successfully. Instead, we've followed the American passion to rely on "the experts" in child rearing, as we have in almost every other area. Thus parents have often wound up feeling insecure and unqualified for their natural biological roles!

By contrast, the "Roots" study provided an opportunity for the natural experts—parents—to expound on things they did well, tapping a rich vein of information and experience. The study is valuable and helpful if it does nothing more than reaffirm the validity of our own inborn parental instincts—something many of us forget in this world of specialists.

One of the unfortunate by-products of our recent obsession with personal fulfillment and self-expression is that nurturing roles such as child care have come to seem of small consequence. Jokes are even made about this. In one, a woman tells other guests at a dinner party that she works for a lawyer and his five children. Everyone is eager to hear how she got such an unusual job; when she finally admits she's married to him and is the children's mother, their faces fall.

It appears, on the surface at least, that many mothers have gloried in their newfound freedom to develop other aspects of themselves, happy to be in a culture where they have the time, money, energy, and social climate to do so. The truth is, as therapists, social workers, and others have learned from years of counseling, they are all still deeply concerned with their parenting responsibilities—even if they're scared by them—and profoundly moved when they find that they do things, as parents, that work.

Motivation—a central question of the study

We've all heard the clichés: If you want something badly enough, you'll get it; dedication is the secret to accomplishment; God helps those who help themselves; and so on. What these adages are really about is motivation—the drive or, as social scientists say, "the need to achieve." We have to remember that in raising successful—or any other—children, we're working with a combination of: (1) what's given at birth—the child's genetic package with all its possibilities, both positive and negative; (2) what we, as parents, can do to "accentuate the positive and eliminate the negative"; and (3) what will ultimately make the youngster want to accentuate the positive for himself—make him want to do the best job, to be the best person, to succeed at whatever the task is, whether it's running a lemonade stand or the state of Kansas.

This last item is motivation. The object of the study, in terms of motivation, was to learn how to make your youngster eager to achieve *for his own sake*, happy in his achievements, confident in his ability to achieve. Note the italics—it's not hard to get a child to finish his homework when *you* have the car and the tickets to the circus. Getting him or her to want to do it on his own is the secret, the one that pays off over a lifetime. We wanted to know how these mothers had done it; from the results it appears that instilling this feeling starts early, and is a lifelong process, with the child ultimately taking over and becoming his own motivator.

Motivation is a complex question; many factors are involved. Genetic inheritance, of course, plays a part. So can adversity in childhood, causing a youngster to learn to rely on his own resources early. Some children are inspired to imitate a parent or other adult; others are propelled by the urge *not* to be like their parents. Cultural, geographical, social, and economic environments may predispose a child toward interest in the outdoors, machines, finance, science, music, art, or other goal, and inspire him to pursue it forcefully to achievement. Plain old energy, as social critic and former Cabinet member John Gardner pointed out, is involved too. He wrote that "Motivation isn't a fuel that gets injected into the system. It is an attribute of individuals, in part linked to their physical vitality, in part a result of social forces—patterns of child rearing, the tone of the educational system, presence or absence of opportunity, the tendency of the society to release or smother available energy, social attitudes toward dedication or commitment, and the vitality of the society's shared values."

Here's how the subject—and the mystery—of motivation was raised in the *Family Circle* study:*

When Kenneth was small, he and his younger brother lived with their parents in Enterprise, Ala., where his father was a $10-a-week butcher and his mother did domestic work. After the family moved north to improve their lot, the four of them lived for five years in a one-room apartment in Newark, N.J. Kenneth's parents couldn't afford to give him many advantages, and there were the additional problems that come with being black in a white society. But despite these difficulties, Kenneth Gibson graduated from

---

*Throughout the book we'll be quoting from the study, usually as italicized matter not attributed to other sources.

college, went into city government and is now mayor of Newark.

When Dorothy Faye was 15, her parents separated and she and her brother lived in Florida with their mother, who worked as a clerk-typist. Dorothy Faye entered college on a state scholarship, transferred to Boston University to study theater and is known today as actress Faye Dunaway.

Most of us think success stories like these are rare, but such dramatic achievements are actually fairly common. Nearly one out of three American boys grows up to hold a more prestigious job than his father had; and one out of every 10 sons of manual workers rises to the highest vocational levels—doctors, lawyers, company presidents. What's the secret? Why should one person climb far up the ladder while another never gets beyond the very bottom rung?

Luck and plain ability play a part, of course. But an individual's personality and character determine whether opportunities will be used or frittered away, whether abilities will be developed or allowed to lie fallow. It is helpful, then, to discover the source of traits that ultimately lead to success—to find, as it were, the roots of success.

Sigmund Freud, who rose from relative obscurity to great renown, was one of the first to suggest that whether a child became a brilliant success or a dismal failure depended largely upon his experiences in the first six years of life. For Freud, literally all behavior had some hidden meaning, some deeper purpose. For example, people who work hard and achieve success suffer from deep feelings of inferiority. According to Freud, their success compensates for real or imagined failures and thereby justifies their existence.

This theory isn't popular with all psychologists today, but it did start researchers wondering about the origins of success and exploring factors that might be important: birth order, socio-economic status of the parents, and so on. Research results, complex and diffuse, do not allow for simplistic, ready-made answers. But a great many studies do point to the importance of the child's day-to-day interactions with his or her parents, particularly the mother.

Mother's contribution and the Pollyanna effect

Obviously, since the survey was addressed to mothers, a critical question was what they had contributed to their famous child's success. This question was asked in a number of ways, as you can see from the copy of the questionnaire which appears in the Appendix. We checked the different responses on each questionnaire for consistency. Indeed, not only were the mothers consistent with themselves in their answers, many agreed with each other:

> A number of women denied any part in their offsprings' achievements ... Many seemed to agree with the great humanist, Dr. Abraham Maslow, who wrote that "a parent cannot make his child into anything. Children make themselves into something."
> Mrs. Gibson, for instance, feels that she had little to do with Kenneth's success. "He did it himself," she insisted. The mother of best-selling author Michael Crichton answered emphatically, "His accomplishments are really his."
> Composer-performer Paul Simon's mother answered simply, "I think it's in his genes." "I don't feel that I deserve any credit for my son's accomplishments," responded the mother of a senator from the Midwest.
> But the bulk of our evidence argues against such modesty. In fact, the questionnaire responses convinced us that parents *can* contribute to the success of their children, that they *do* play a vital role in shaping a child's future. Of course, the mothers' recollections may have been distorted by time. Psychologists Margaret Matlin and David Stang have documented what they call the "Pollyanna effect," the tendency of people to exaggerate the best and minimize the

worst when recalling the past. This general tendency helps us to bury painful memories, remaining optimistic and cheerful in the present—and certainly contributes to our health. We can't assume that these mothers were any more immune to this phenomenon than the rest of us. In fact, some of our respondents raised the issue themselves. As one mother told us in an interview, "As the years go by, we mothers are apt to glamorize." But the pattern that emerged from their comments and their answers to the questionnaire was so consistent from mother to mother that we can't simply dismiss it as coincidence.

Beyond that, the mothers who returned the questionnaire must be regarded as a particular category among all the mothers we contacted. They were either the proudest of their child-rearing acomplishments, or the most willing to help—or both. For our purposes this sample was ideal, for we were eager to learn—from mothers who were well satisfied—what seemed to be the most outstanding features of their children's early years. And they were willing to tell us.

What, no problems?

For all their modesty and pride, these mothers admitted to many problems, and talked about how they coped. They spoke of many fine parents who try hard, seem to do everything right, and still have children who fail to live up to their potential, or who suffer emotional or other hardships. Many of the mothers had experienced this in their own families, where siblings of the achieving child had a tougher time, although they were being raised in an environment similar to that of the child who grew up to be a star. Nothing could speak more eloquently of the roll-of-the-dice aspect of raising a successful child, as many other mothers poignantly observed.

Nevertheless, we feel that their behaviors and attitudes suggest a pattern of handling life that enabled them to deal better with inevitable problems. Despite all the other factors that influence success, these mothers seem to have held at least some of the keys to it—and to have used them.

2. The earth for the roots: the achievers' backgrounds

In looking at the survey sample, it's interesting to note details such as religious faith, size of family, birth order, geographical location, parents' backgrounds and so on. These are all factors against which we can compare our own situations to see how they match or differ. There are also less obvious factors, some of those "social forces" John Gardner mentioned in his description of motivation—conducive climate for success (he called it "presence or absence of opportunity"), shared values, and the like.

A second area we looked at was the developmental histories of the achievers: at what ages they walked, talked, showed their talents or gifts.

To our mixed delight (as parents) and dismay (as researchers), there were no consistent answers on either front. Certainly some factors were shared by a majority of the achievers—for instance, a surprising 70 percent of the mothers had some college education—but there were always others, usually a healthy number (such as the 30 percent who did not go to college), who did *not* share the trait.

What this suggests is that, genetic factors aside, superstars are made, not born. Thus the ball is back in mother's—and child's—court. As you read through this material to see where factors occur in your situation that might seem favorable or can be worked with, just remember that with these matters there are no right answers.

Age, sex, ethnic background, and the climate for success

These factors are all connected, and taken together, can play an important role. If one grows up in an environment where achievement is on the agenda, everyone will be doing it. There will not only be a climate of acceptance for the effort, there will be criticism for not making it. The reverse seems also to be true.

Looking at the sample, we see that most of the achievers are now between thirty-five and fifty years old, which means they grew up between the late 1930s and early 1960s, a period when the white male was the undisputed leader in virtually every area of achievement save child rearing. Though it wasn't in our minds when we put together the sample, this climate of success for white males is certainly reflected in it. Seventy-two percent of the achievers are men, 28 percent women—compared with the almost 50:50 ratio for the national population. The figure for blacks in the survey—13 percent—is closer but still below the national rate, which is 15 percent for all nonwhite population.

A couple of interesting illustrations bear this out. A study in *Fortune* magazine on the heads of the Fortune 500 (the 500 biggest corporations in the country) reported that for years they have been men who were overwhelmingly WASP (White Anglo-Saxon Protestant) and socially "right," right down to their Republican leanings and Episcopalian religion. Now more of them are coming from lower-middle-class and Catholic, Jewish, and Lutheran backgrounds; but the typical Fortune 500 chief "is still a he and white as well; only one woman, Katharine Graham of the *Washington Post*, and no blacks have reached this corporate altitude." (It's well known that Katharine Graham inherited the newspaper from her father, and undertook its management when her husband, who had been its chief, died. She has since passed the reins to her son.)

Compare this to the story of Dr. May Chinn, who is truly a testament to the power of motivation. In a recent *New York Times* article about her, George Davis described Dr. Chinn, now close to ninety, as the first black woman graduate of Bellevue Hospital Medical College (now New York University's medical school), the first black woman intern at Harlem Hospital, the first black woman to practice medicine in Harlem. So bleak was the climate for this kind of person doing this kind of work that according to Davis, "one well-intentioned white male doctor even urged May to go to China as a medical missionary and learn the language there. Then she could pass herself off as Chinese and circumvent some of the discrimination a black doctor, much less a black woman doctor, would inevitably run up against."

Happily for women, blacks, and other minorities, the climate for success is changing rapidly for the better. This is something parents of such children may want to keep in mind. Until now, these children really had to overcome heavy odds just to get into the race, much less win it. Parents of white male children may want to consider the changing picture too, since it appears there's going to be competition coming in from new quarters.

Parents' backgrounds and education

Most of the survey parents were born in the U. S., and most of them came from the Midwest or Northeast (about 30 percent each). About 15 percent more came from the South, 10 percent from the West. Almost 20 percent of the fathers and 10 percent of the mothers were born abroad, however. Except in homes where the foreign-born parent came from Canada, there's the strong likelihood that another language—or at least another accent—was heard around the house. About 65 percent of the mothers grew up in cities or towns of 100,000 or more; another 25 percent came from small towns or farms; the rest from suburbs.

Educational levels, as we've noted, were unusually high for the parent group: 70 percent of the mothers and 67 percent of the fathers had at least some time at college. This was very high for women in a period when relatively few went past high school. Even by 1977, according to census figures, only 15 percent of all American adults were completing college, which means for the women, who amount to half the college population, the figure is less than 10 percent. So this was an impressively educated parent group for its time. However, don't forget that 30 percent of the mothers and 33 percent of the fathers had no college—and managed to raise superstars anyway.

Parents' occupations

The fathers' occupations ranged from pharmacist to artist, from cattle dealer to biochemist. A startling 17 percent were lawyers, many of whose wives worked too. The largest group were white-collar men, working in advertising, sales, insurance, and so on; then came the lawyers; then skilled laborers; then educators; and finally the arts. About 60 percent of the mothers worked, most in typical womens' jobs of the period: secretary, clerk-typist, administrative assistant, teacher. Almost half the working mothers taught, ranging from teaching music at home to lecturing at universities. A few owned their own businesses, operated restaurants, and so on. A good many did volunteer work outside the home. We discuss these working mothers throughout the book in relation to their present-day counterparts.

Religious faith, social class, income

Just as *Fortune* magazine could have predicted, about 50 percent of the survey families were Protestant; 23 percent Jewish; 15 percent Catholic, the rest answered "other" or "none" to the question of religious background.

There's some interesting research on this subject. David McClelland, a noted social scientist who pioneered the work on motivation and the drive to achieve, found that Protestant and Jewish families expected greater independence, which is linked to motivation, from their children than did families of other faiths. McClelland had defined this motivation/drive as "the need to achieve" and further research showed that Protestant children scored very highly on tests for the need to achieve.

McClelland's work also showed that in most religious groups there's a correlation between the family's income and social class, and its emphasis on achievement: The higher the class, the greater the emphasis. The exception was Jewish families, where they all, regardless of income, stressed achievement.

McClelland felt that a family's moving up, in terms of class and income, was a powerful reinforcement for achievement in children. Though the income of the survey families while they were raising their children varied from below $5,000 per year to well over $20,000, about 75 percent of the families at all levels reported that they moved up during this child-rearing period, just as McClelland's theory would suggest.

There's abundant evidence on the contrasting negative effects of poverty. Kenneth Keniston, chairman of the Carnegie Council on Children, believes this is chiefly because poverty—and all the problems that go with it—take the parents' energy and attention away from the children just when their responsiveness and enthusiasm are most needed to help the children develop. Sadly, he says that "about 25 percent of all American children grow up today in conditions of economic hardship that are really damaging to them and their families." Nevertheless, some of our achievers came from very poor families where there was apparently enough energy and spirit left over to give them the will not only to survive, but to succeed.

Urban/rural environment

Like their mothers, most of the achievers grew up in cities or towns. About 25 percent also, like mother, came from small towns or rural areas; but another 25 percent, more than twice as many as in mother's day, came from the suburbs.

More than one mother who raised her children in a small town or suburb said she wished she'd brought them up in a big city. We speculated that the stimulation of an urban environment might be important for achievers, or that families drawn to cities might be more restless and achievement-oriented than country folk who stay put. Indeed, it turned out that thirty years ago, when the survey children were growing up, the 25 percent of the survey group who were rural dwellers were well below the 44 percent of the national population who were rural.

Family stability

Although maintaining marriages and stable family structure was much more common in the survey children's time than it is now, this was still noteworthy in the sample:

> *... most of our successes issue from unusually robust and stable families. When we asked whether the mothers had been separated, divorced, or widowed while their children were growing up, only 16 percent said yes. The divorce rate alone for this generation should have been from somewhere between 25 percent and 33 percent, judging by the figures for the general population.*
>
> *The only group that approached these figures was Entertainment: a third of these mothers had been separated, divorced, or widowed while their youngsters were growing up. In fact, if we omit the Entertainment group from our calculations, the overall figure for early domestic disruption, including separation, divorce, and death, is only 10 percent.*

Even when father had to be away—22 percent reported absences of six months to three years—the family stayed together. Many of these were WW II-related absences, but it should also be remembered that the social climate during the period the survey children were being raised heavily favored stability and disapproved of divorce. Being a child of a broken home implied something was amiss. There hasn't been time yet to determine how marital breakups will affect children who are growing up in today's world, where the social climate is much more accepting of all kinds of marital/parental arrangements, and the single-parent household is becoming commonplace.

Size of family

Most of the families were small. About 60 percent had only one or two children; 20 percent, three children; 10 percent, four children; the rest, five or more children. However, this was a time when families tended to be small. Two world wars kept men away from home, and many Depression couples had reservations about having children at all. The theory about firstborns described below suggests that the smallness of the families helped the achievers. In economically pressed homes, it certainly eases the strain if there are fewer mouths to feed.

Considering that fully 40 percent of the achievers came from families with three or more children, however, there's evidence supporting larger families too. People from large families often remember warmly the mutual support and closeness they felt in growing up in such a group. Country-western singer Dolly Parton, one of twelve children, has made her experience famous in many of her songs. In the survey group there were several families like that of Atlanta Mayor Maynard Jackson, where all six children are highly accomplished; or psychobiologist Sarah Fryer Leibowitz, with five. Author George Plimpton, Senator Daniel Moynihan, and scientist Joel Cohen all came from families with four or more children.

Firstborn and only children

An interesting, but predictable, finding was the prevalence of firstborn and only children among the achievers. They comprised 60 percent of the sample. A multitude of research has shown that firstborns seem to achieve. Here's one theory why:

> *Behavioral scientist Robert B. Zajonc of the University of Michigan argues that the firstborn child enters a world of adults and thus receives the richest intellectual stimulation the parents can provide. But each successive child reduces the parents' time and other resources, and the intellectual level of the home declines. The researcher speculates that this is why the oldest is often the brightest child in the family. It is also why, in study after study of successful people, a large proportion of them turn out to be either firstborn or only children.*

Twenty-eight of the survey children were firstborn—twenty-one boys and seven girls. Seven more were only children.

One, Congresswoman Elizabeth Holtzman, was a firstborn "supertwin": Her brother's now a noted neurosurgeon.

- *Firstborn sons* There's also specific evidence about firstborn sons. They're predominant in *Who's Who;* twenty-one of the original twenty-three astronauts were firstborn; there's a high number of firstborn sons in executive ranks. Four more members of the sample were the first boys born in their families. In families where males are expected to do the achieving and females to fill more passive roles, this is almost as significant a placement as being a firstborn son.

- *Firstborn daughters* Although when these parents were raising their children, most girls were headed for domestic roles, some did groom their daughters for other accomplishments. Margot Hennig, author of *The Managerial Woman*, has shown, as have others, that many women in the upper levels of management today were actively coached by their fathers to follow in their footsteps. Hennig located one hundred women corporate presidents and vice-presidents in her research. *All* were firstborns.

    In support of these theories, intelligence tests given to four hundred thousand teenagers showed that regardless of the size of the family, firstborns consistently scored better than later-borns, and that test scores tended to fall in relation to (1) birth order, and (2) the number of children in the family (the more children, the lower the scores).

    Other studies have shown similar results, but it remains to be explained why only children do not do as well as firstborns. Perhaps, as one theory suggests, it's because they have no peers to consult with close to their own level in the home.

Younger and last-born children

Younger siblings in the family seem to have a different advantage. Studies show that last-born children tend to be more popular as playmates, while firstborns are most often selected by their friends to achieve a certain objective. The firstborn child is alone with his playthings and pursuits in the company of "goal-directed" adults, who are going about getting things started and finished, something the child can't help noticing. He is relatively free of relationships with other children, at least for a time, while the last-born grows up in the company of siblings from his earliest object-relationships, as Freudians call our first attachment to things beyond ourselves. Twenty percent of the survey sample were last borns: Seven were the youngest of two children; three the youngest of three; one the youngest of five.

These birth-order theories are interesting to think about; but again, as we can see, they are not consistently reflected in the survey sample. Instead, the evidence leads us to agree with Dr. Julius Segal at the National Institute of Mental Health, who said "Birth order doesn't stand alone as being an indicator of how well a child will do in life. It is likely to be subtle and less consequential by far than the impact of the basic parental attitudes, values and behaviors that are palpable to the child in the family environment, no matter what his or her place in the hierarchy of siblings."

This is certainly more consistent with our feeling when we look at how the survey parents coped with life's challenges, regardless of family size, birth order, religion, or race.

Timing

A number of mothers spoke of *timing* in relation to their children's success. Older parents had seen the Depression erode the ambitions of their older children, while their younger children—coming along later—had had much greater opportunities. But a still later generation of parents spoke of their older children's good fortune in preceding the sixties, before the drug culture and social unrest which sidetracked younger children from their goals.

It is clear from all this data that there is no one factor or group of factors that makes for success. No doubt all the factors played a subtle role. You can compare them with your own circumstances. Certainly changed since the survey mothers raised their children, are the social forces, such as the climate for success, which is expanding, and the maintenance of stable family structure, which is dwindling. We'll be discussing how these and other factors have an effect on the rearing of an achiever today.

Were superstars supertots?

This is the developmental picture, and here again we found no overwhelming trends. We realized it was asking a lot to expect the mothers to remember their children's first words or steps, and that they might exaggerate somewhat in looking back, but we still felt that their answers would show us a pattern of precocity, if there was one. However, the superstars did not show, as a group, accelerated mental or physical development as infants, nor did they all stand out as gifted at early ages, though some certainly did.

• Physical development *About 50 percent of the children started crawling as early as six months of age; the next 30 percent crawled at between 9 and 12 months, about average for this skill. [The rest were later than that. This puts them, as a group, ahead of, on, and behind the norm.] One superstar began walking, if his mother's memory serves, at about six months—an impressive accomplishment indeed. But over 40 percent of the children didn't walk until they were about a year old, the approximate time when most children begin to walk. Three* children (two of whom later became scholars or scientists) did not toddle until they were about a year-and-a-half, considered a little late.

If we take crawling and walking as indicators of physical maturation, then this group impresses for its lack of uniformity in development. This is consistent, though, with other research showing that physical development in infancy and early childhood has very little to do with later measures of ability.

• Speaking and reading *The age at which children speak and read is a somewhat better indicator of later performance, and some superstars were indeed precocious in these skills. But once again the group was precocious* and *uneven. We asked the mothers when their children started to speak in complete sentences, and about 60 percent of those responding said their child started putting words into short sentences before the age of two. [Most of the rest] thought their supertots reached this point in their second or third year, when most children acquire the skill.*

We got similar results when we inquired about reading. Three children read by the time they were two. In all, twenty-one mothers, nearly half of those responding to this question, said that their child read by age four. [One was reading Thomas Mann at seven.] On the other hand, twenty-three didn't begin to read until they were five or more—about the age most children start reading. And some of those who showed no special signs of precocity in reading are now top scientists or famous writers.

So while some superstars seemed to be born with special abilities that might have made later success easy for them, many others showed no early signs of unusual talent. Since heredity is partly responsible for a person's abilities and may even help shape certain personality traits, it is *a factor in success. But the fact that many of our superstars weren't especially gifted as youngsters means that we cannot attribute their later successes only to good genes.*

Timetables for talent: from prodigies to late bloomers

Although the group developed randomly, several children were undeniably precocious. One little girl had held up her head and turned over at two weeks, and had climbed, catapulted, and performed balancing acts by age one. This mother said, not surprisingly, "As a tiny child, she was so apt it was frightening." The same youngster, when older, won all the contests she entered and became a skilled musician by rote, as she couldn't see the music; glasses weren't prescribed for her until much later.

Another youngster "talked in sentences at the age of one." Nobel prizewinner Rosalyn Yalow's mother tells how Rosalyn, staying overnight at her aunt's at age three, mentioned that she didn't know how to tell time, was shown how, and had mastered it by the time she was returned home in the morning. Rosalyn had always seemed bright, but in a family that excelled in arithmetic, not much was thought of it until one of her teachers began to make an issue of it. Graduating from junior high at twelve, high school at sixteen, and college at nineteen, her rate of progress was certainly exceptional.

Writer-producer Michael Crichton was another early science whiz, winning prizes routinely as a youngster, publishing articles as a teenager in national magazines. In medical school, while others were struggling to make it through scholastically and financially, he was paying his tuition by writing whodunits in his spare time.

Yves St. Laurent's mother tells this story: At the age of four, her son "made his aunt change her dress ... at least six times ... before he would let her go out one evening, and he was so sure of himself that we accepted it from him."

This varied rate of progress is common to children who grew up to be in the limelight. Many gifted children are spotted during grade-school years by parents startled by their talents, or by teachers who recognize them as standouts and want to ensure that the best education is provided for them. Our respondents described such children as "exceedingly agile," "very grown-up" for their ages, and so on.

Some gifts seem to appear early in families where parents or siblings are already achievers in the skill. The abilities of such children may simply be recognized sooner because everyone around is watching and cultivating talent so intensely. The Wyeths who paint, the scientific Baranys (mother, father, two sons), and the singing/dancing Guthries come to mind.

More individual bents—those which are independent of family influence and seem to reflect something from within the youngster—frequently turn up in high school, the period when we are, in fact, developing our independence and individuality. Jim Henson—the Muppet man—for instance, had an unremarkable childhood. According to a *Time* story about him, during his senior year in a Maryland high school, he heard that a local TV station was looking for puppeteers. He knew nothing about puppets, but he was fascinated by television, so he and a friend sewed together a rat puppet that "looked French." "Puppetry released something" in Henson, and soon his career was under way "with an ease and certainty that now seem almost eeerie: A nearby NBC station hired 'Pierre and Friends' to help out on a cartoon show"—and the rest is history.

- *The nonprodigy child* Although we've been discussing children who displayed their gifts while still in school, remember that many others appeared unexceptional. Einstein is a famous example. Legend has it that a schoolteacher once told his father, "I fear the boy will never amount to anything."

    By comparison to the norm, Einstein was "slow"—he didn't speak until the age of three. He reportedly tied this to his later achievement in this wonderful explanation: "A normal adult never stops to think about problems of space or time. Most people have thought about these problems when they are children. But my intellectual development was slow, and so I did not start to think about space and time until I was already grown up. Consequently, I went into those problems more thoroughly than a child would."

The most famous long-term study of achievers ever done brought out the same point about hidden gifts. Known as the Terman Study, after its originator Lewis Terman, it has followed over 1,500 high-IQ people since the 1920's, when most of them were California schoolchildren. Although the group has done better than most of its peers in life, not one artistic or creative genius emerged from it—"no Einsteins, no Picassos" observed one report—suggesting that the divine spark does indeed lie beyond what IQ or other predictive tests might turn up at early ages.

Many very great achievers—especially those gifted in management, law, politics, medicine—don't show their gifts until later, in adulthood, when they've found an arena where their skills can be expressed, such as the corporation, courtroom, or operating theater. Hence, if your youngster is not an obvious prodigy, drawing like Rembrandt at age two, composing like Mozart at four, or leading the debating team at five, don't assume abilities aren't there or won't flower. Our mothers showed faith in their children's futures that often proved out long after childhood.

- *Choice of field* This may also influence the age at which one becomes successful. Rock and television stars now surface at twelve or thirteen, and movie stars can hit the top at the ripe old age of twenty-four, as John Travolta did. The youthful business executive is increasingly in demand. Science and scholarship, like many professions, tend to reward the veteran of twenty to thirty years of effort; this age group is where one finds the prizewinners, the department chiefs, principal speakers at professional meetings, and so on. Politics usually requires at least some wisdom of the statesman: The higher the office, the older the candidate.

The earth for the roots

- *Late bloomers* It is becoming more common to achieve later in life, despite theories that most of us peak in our thirties and then mellow, passing our skills and wisdom to others—apprentices, students, protégés—in our forties and fifties.

The theories may have been right for their time, but there are changes in the air. The Women's Movement gave many women the permission they were seeking to bloom, albeit late, and thousands have developed career competence and creativity in their thirties and forties after child rearing. Men and women alike have come increasingly to realize that they can change their lives in midlife and beyond, even after retirement, and now midlife personal, domestic, and career changes are quite usual.

A classic late bloomer is Barbara Tuchman. Describing herself in a *New York Times* article as "a late developer," she was fifty when *The Guns of August* became a huge bestseller. It has been followed by a series of equally impressive books. She says that her family, including her husband, "never took me seriously until I was famous, and it is my greatest sorrow that my parents died before I became important."

Although this book is filled with what mothers and fathers did and can do to foster achievers, this touching remark shows the other side of the equation: how deeply achievers—like all of us—feel about impressing and pleasing our parents no matter how grown-up we may be.

3. Gifted mothering: the three-fold commitment

We've seen that most of our superstars were unremarkable as babies and that their backgrounds vary so much as to be inconclusive. So beyond admitting that genes play a part, we want to talk about what *was* striking: the evidence of what mother can contribute to raising an achiever from a very early age. Almost without exception, the mothers of our superstars took a very intense and serious interest in the child, observing and nurturing his or her talents and abilities early. Beyond cuddling and loving, they watched to see how the child responded to music, pictures, building blocks. One mother took her child, now a world-famous performing artist, for musical training at the age of two; many mothers began to read to their infants by the age of one.

This type of early interest crossed all socioeconomic backgrounds and always involved the mother, sometimes the father or other relatives. Instead of a group of gifted child prodigies, what we found was a group of gifted mothers. Consistencies that didn't turn up in the backgrounds or development patterns of the survey children did begin to emerge in the responses and attitudes of their otherwise diverse mothers. Basically, this gifted mothering seemed to rest on a deep commitment to the child from the beginning which was sustained throughout the child's upbringing. The mothers were also consistent in *not* laying their own aspirations on the child, but rather in encouraging his or her own bent, often in what seemed self-sacrificing ways.

The threefold commitment

Since over half the survey mothers worked at some point during their child-rearing years, we are not talking about self-sacrificing enslavement to the child when we say commitment, but rather a point of view, one that anyone raising children could take—and take advantage of. In looking over the answers from the mothers, this point of view seemed to consist of three main components:

1. Expectation of greatness and belief in the child's future. This was the idea, sometimes fixed upon before the child was born, that he or she would have ability and could "go places."

2. Intense involvement, especially in the early years. This was displayed by nearly all the mothers, and was the core of the child-rearing process. Critical factors contributing to future achievement—such as establishing trust, providing stimulation, setting standards, and so on—were set in place through this involvement.

3. Early recognition and enthusiastic support of the child's gifts and interests. This was usually born out of the mother's first bringing all kinds of stimulation to the child, sometimes, as we've seen, as early as the second or third year. A most important aspect was continued unswerving loyalty and support of the child.

These three components all relate directly to the mother's "plugging in" to the child as a person in his or her own right, from the beginning. Each stage grew out of and reinforced the previous one: Because of their high expectations, the mothers became intensely involved with their children, watching their growth and their response to things. Because of the intense involvement, it was possible for them to spot talent early. Having identified it, their expectations and supportive attitude made them willing to foster it. What seemed to be going on with the survey mothers was that, from babyhood, each felt her child was *already a person with a promising future* and that while this future was in her care, she was going to see that it had every opportunity to thrive.

Expectation of greatness and belief in the child's future

This idea is immediately expressed in the cliche of the new mother cooing down at her infant, "Someday you'll be..." (President, quarterback of the Rams, first woman conductor of the symphony). This pinning of adult hopes and joys on the newborn is one of the cornerstones of child rearing—it keeps mothers going through some of the difficult times. But when does a child actually become a person in the mind of his parents, an identity on whom they *can* pin hopes?

Research as well as everyday experience shows that it's long before birth. Even in the early weeks of pregnancy, the parents' attitudes toward the coming child are expressed through nicknames and private jokes until finally they choose a name that officially identifies the baby.

Gifted mothering 33

- *Given names* Although achievers bear every kind of name, we learned that some interesting research had been done on the relationship between children's first names and how they perceive themselves and are perceived by others. Quizzing children, their classmates, and their teachers on names suggested that children with common and well-accepted names may be rated more highly in some situations. In one study, children with such names scored higher on standardized tests and had a stronger concept of themselves as achievers. We checked this theory against our sample, and indeed, 85 percent had names like John, Elizabeth, William, Barbara, and so on. This is no guarantee of success, however, since most people have such names. Perhaps it's more interesting to note that Twyla, Chevy, and Faye achieved admirably with less than common names—as have many others.

- *Dreams of glory* Naming the new baby is only one indication of the parents' feelings about it. There's much more to the story, as Robert Sears, Eleanor Maccoby, and Harry Levin describe in their book *Patterns of Child Rearing:*

    It is not altogether obvious where one should start in describing the rearing of a child. The least ambiguous point might be the moment of birth, or better still, the instant at which the mother first sees her baby. But a great deal has already gone on before this time. The parents have made preparations and developed expectations. They have begun to live a new kind of life, in an anticipatory way. Their reactions to the imminence of parenthood are inevitably influenced by certain qualities of their own individual personalities. And the attitudes that they have toward the child at his birth are an important part of his social and emotional environment....

    Fantasies about the future may be part of every family's hopes for its newborn, but for the mothers of achievers they were more than just fantasies. When asked how important it was for their child to grow up "to attain a standard of excellence or high achievement," no less than 71 percent gave this the highest rating of "very important." In response to questions like "what was your greatest contribution to your child's success?" they offered answers such as these:

"I always believed in my children, had a dream for them, backed them up—and I still do."

"Providing love and security at home, giving her independence and freedom to pursue the course she most wanted, and faith in her ability to succeed."

"Being interested in her, and loving her and her future."

Each mother's anticipation that her child could or would do well rested on the unspoken conviction: *if given the right opportunities and attention.* As natural an understanding as bringing a little plant home from the store: Put it in the right window, give it plenty of water and fertilizer, and it'll grow for you. Leave it in its bag in the corner, and it won't make it—nor would you expect it to. Quite innocently, many mothers who are clearly solicitous toward a helpless plant's simplest needs for survival fail to see or accommodate the same basic needs for nurturing, stimulation, and encouragement in their own offspring.

It's a twofold premise: The mothers believed that (1) their children could do well, and (2) their own efforts could make a difference; so they made those efforts in order to make that difference. There is ample evidence to support their contention.

- *Effect of parental expectations on children* We've been speaking of the expectation of greatness as a component of gifted mothering, but of course it has undeniably compelling effects on children. A great many achievers remember this as being critical to their motivation. A college professor, though not one of our sample, believed one of the most valuable gifts he received from his parents was "the sense I could do what I wanted to do." Daniel Callahan, cofounder

of The Hastings Center said, "There was an expectation that one would do well, and exceed one's parents.... I was brought up in such a way that I had a sense of competence; that I would do good things eventually."
Many others had similar feelings of being fated to do something worthwhile. A writer: "I believed I could do anything I wanted to, well. My parents were extremely supportive. I even believed I could be an opera singer if I wanted to." A scientist: "I never saw myself as anything else. Later on I had doubts along the way, but never as a child—my parents made it clear that I could do it."
We all remember doing things to please our parents and earn their love and respect. Barbara Tuchman's remark at the end of the last chapter is only one evidence of this, and as we'll read later, many of the superachieving children still have a strong sense of family or family feeling.
There are two sides to this question. On the one hand, having high hopes and expectations seems to have a beneficial effect on children, as we can see from the remarks above. The article described the following research confirming this:

Dr. Robert Rosenthal conducted studies of the effects teachers' attitudes have on students. He found that when teachers expected a student to progress rapidly, he or she usually did so; when teachers expected a child to lag behind, those expectations also were likely to be met.

If teachers' attitudes can affect students' academic performances, it is reasonable to believe that the same kind of self-fulfilling prophecy works at home. Parents who expect a child to fail may be inviting problems.

This is, in fact, well known to be true; and the literature of child guidance is filled with evidence of the "scapegoat" or "problem child" role in the family constellation—the youngster who *always* gets it wrong, does it wrong, *is* wrong. A great deal of time and effort goes into reversing both the problem child's and the family's low expectations in such cases.

On the other hand, high expectations should not be confused with being hypercritical and overdemanding, which can have damaging long-term effects dating from an amazingly early age. Researchers Earl Schaefer and Nancy Bayley wrote of this after studying the effects of maternal behavior on children, using intelligence tests as guides to progress over a time span.

They found that daughters of loving and controlling mothers had high IQs for the first three years of life; but after three, there were no strong correlations between mothers and girl babies. (Other studies have indicated that fathers may have greater influence over daughters after infancy.) Schaefer and Bayley's findings for boys, however, were definitive. Mothers who evaluated their boy babies positively gave them affection, granted them autonomy (letting them do some exploring and finding out on their own) and equality, and had infant sons who were happy and calm but scored *below average* on mental tests for the first year of life. Hostile, punitive mothers had active, unhappy, excitable boy babies who scored *above average* for one-year-olds. By age five, however, the story was different. The happy, calm low-scorers had covered so much ground that they were now more likely to have high IQs, whereas the others now scored low on tests. This was an important finding, as it's generally felt that IQ levels stabilize for life at around age four.

The Schaefer-Bayley research also included observation of the mothers. The mothers of the later high-scorers tended to show emotional involvement, concern about their child's health, and demand for achievement—in other words, high expectations and belief that the child should, and could, accomplish things on his own. In contrast, the mothers of the later low-scorers displayed intrusiveness, anxiety, irritability, use of fear and punishment, strictness,

Gifted mothering

perception of the child as a burden, and a tendency to ignore the child.

You can see from this that demand for achievement and high expectations throughout the child-rearing process are critically, though not obviously, different from being controlling and dominating. This is one of the great balancing acts of parenthood, and much in this book relates to how the survey mothers handled it. Their remarks suggest they made plenty of demands, but somehow managed always to mix in some support or encouragement. This evidently began at a very early age, and certainly continued through adolescence; probably into adulthood. Chevy Chase's mother said she had always "showed open admiration for her son's accomplishments." Dr. Sarah Leibowitz's mother said her daughter had grown up in "an achievement-oriented family where talents and interests were encouraged." Faye Dunaway's mother remembered "a constant pounding of a 'can do' philosophy."

Mothers like Faye Dunaway's are a familiar type in these accounts. Her daughter described her in a recent article as "the spunkiest woman I've ever met...She was not a stage mother by any means, but she was totally seduced by what you'd call the American Dream—to raise yourself in the world, to go beyond what everybody in our world was doing. My brother and I were the only two in our family to finish college....The American Dream is, 'You can be from the wrong side of the tracks but you can make it, kid.'"

This expectation and belief-in-the-future attitude was consistent almost throughout the entire sample, no matter what area—politics, the arts, business—the child grew to succeed in. These ideas often emerge in other accounts of mothers. Mike Douglas, reminiscing on his television show one day, said "My mother played a large role in my success; she always used to say 'I can't' is for failures." Probably the most famous of all is Abraham Lincoln's "All that I am...I owe to my darling mother."

May Chinn, the Harlem physician we met in the last

chapter, had an amazingly determined mother, who was the child of an Indian mother and a former slave father. Lulu Chinn started work as a domestic at fifteen, later became a cook on a wealthy estate, and devoted her life to educating her only child: "The sole purpose of her working was to see me through school. She wanted me to get a college degree...." And when May was accepted at college and her father was "not impressed," her mother "reached into her bosom and pulled out a piece of cloth. She unknotted it and counted out four hundred dollars on the kitchen table. Secretly, she had been saving money all this time....Not only did Lulu provide the money for May to go to college; she also moved the family from the Bronx to Harlem so May could walk to classes."

Nothing further need be said about the power of a mother's dream for the ultimate success of her offspring.

Intense involvement, especially in the early years

There seemed no question that the survey mothers were deeply involved with their children. Hand in hand with their expectations that their children would do well was their willingness to put the children first in their own lives. They spent time with them, talked to them, played with them, held and hugged them; and as the years went by, continued to pay a great deal of attention to them. As the article noted,

> *Our data left no doubt that the relationships between our high achievers and their mothers was very special indeed. These mothers seemed to have been more than just fond of their children. They were preoccupied, almost obsessed, by an interest in their offspring "I was interested in anything he was interested in," Paul Simon's mother confided. And Tessie Jamison, mother of dancer Judith*

Jamison, told about her "concern and care and constant support [of] her interests."

The mothers in our study made a point of being readily available to their children. The words "being there" surfaced again and again when mothers were asked how they had helped their children. "Letting her know I was always there to talk to," said the mother of a prominent political scientist. "Simply being present when he needed me," answered another.

"To be there when needed and give all the love and guidance I could," remembered Dionne Warwick's mother. Theologian Alfred Gottschalk's said "closeness and trust" had been her offering. The list goes on and on, and this "being there" and closeness were regardless of the other pulls and responsibilities of the mothers' lives. Kenneth Gibson's mother, who worked from the time her children were tiny, recalls how her boys would climb into bed with her to talk first thing in the morning, after their father left for work and before she did. Dr. Kate Barany, a scientist who is married to a scientist and has raised two sons in science, was already deeply involved in her work when her boys were young, but she telephoned her children every morning, and returned from work at three so she could spend an hour alone with each of them. Both children speak of this to this day.

Closeness was the thing that was emphasized, whether the mothers were at work or home-based, as Don Kirschner's was. This is especially important to keep in mind today, when many women are taking time out from careers to have children instead of the other way around. Granting that the time-giving aspect of the survey group's mothering requires adaptation to these new circumstances, it's still important to look at what the data revealed about the quality of the relationship. It was a matter of being together emotionally, knowing what was going on with the child, and knowing what mattered to him. Mrs. Kirschner said simply, "It's knowing if a child is happy."

- *Two factors that help make achievers* Many researchers, starting with Freud, have dealt with the importance of what happens in early childhood as it relates to later life. Our evidence suggests that this early intense involvement of the survey mothers could have positively affected their achieving children in many ways. But two factors—establishing closeness and trust, and providing outside stimulation—can probably do as much as any to make a nongifted child into a happy and achieving one. Not only have both factors been shown to affect IQ, but more important, they help create that sense of inner security that can be a lifelong resource to anyone, especially in making decisions—and mistakes—again and again.

Significance of early closeness and trust: Erikson's stages

This goal of closeness and trust was accomplished by what the mothers called "being there." Establishing trust in a child is one of the great foundation stones of child rearing, according to Erik Erikson, a giant in modern thinking on how children grow. He theorized that there are eight stages in the life-growth process. Each stage embraces a task that must be "accomplished" before we can move on to the next one successfully. Even though we grow in chronological and physical ways, we continue to work on the unfinished business of previous stages throughout our lives. If we don't fully accomplish the task of each stage, according to Erikson, we can develop symptoms associated with this failure, and remain immature in these ways. We can all recognize these symptoms of immaturity within ourselves and others when they appear.

The task of Erikson's first stage is the development of trust, and it rests on "consistency and continuity of handling" and "the quality of the maternal relationship." Further, "Mothers create a sense of trust in their children by that kind of administration which in its quality combines sensitive care of the baby's individual needs and a firm sense of personal trustworthiness." This trust forms the basis in the child of an identity which will later combine with a sense of being "all right," of being oneself, and of becoming what others believe one can become. In the mature individual, trust eventually evolves into a common faith, a sense of the trustworthiness of the human enterprise.

Very simply, if a child is consistently fed and nurtured, secure confidence develops that one *will* be fed, that the world is a good place where one's needs will be attended to without having to ask. These feelings persist into adulthood when, although the need to be fed and nurtured has passed, the need to feel one *will be* has not. Giving your child this deep-rooted emotional security can thus be crucial to his lifelong feelings of faith in the world and in himself. Hence the accomplishment of stage one, basic trust, is the establishment of faith and hope in the individual.

Erikson puts two other stages into this early period: *autonomy* and *initiative*. Autonomy is the beginning exercise of choice. For this, a child needs parental control that is firmly reassuring, so that he may avoid feelings of shame and doubt when he makes a mistake or "does something wrong." This stage is associated with the perils of toilet training, learning to feed oneself, and so on.

Researcher Margaret Mahler added this dimension: Each child experiences a "second birth" at around eighteen months, during this same active or mastering stage, as it's called. Children are not only learning to walk and handle things, but are becoming increasingly aware that they have an identity separate from that of their mothers. They also discover they have a free will of their own, a capacity to make decisions (one reason this stage is sometimes known as the "terrible twos"). In a view parallel to Erikson's, Mahler says that for this second birth—where the child enters the self-conscious world—to be as successful as the first, where he entered the physical world, also requires a consistent emotional relationship with the mother or mother figure. That is, the person should be the same, and should be acting in the same way toward the child before, during, and after this milestone: Erikson's "consistency and continuity of handling."

For working mothers/single parents it's important to note that this "mother figure" can be a parent or adult of either sex; what is crucial is the solidity and constancy of the relationship itself, which gives the infant its feeling of safety and security.

Psychologist Louise Kaplan also deals with this transition in her recent book *Oneness and Separateness*. As the toddler reaches this mastering stage, Kaplan recommends granting considerable autonomy and showing tolerance of his attempts to find things out on his own (even if it means finding out that feeding oneself involves more hair and hand than it does spoon and mouth), along with making reasonable demands for mastery of these tasks—the first forms of achievement and accomplishment.

Kaplan's feeling, also like Erikson's, is that if a child is too closely restricted and controlled during this period, he or she may emerge from the second birth with a "pervasive sense of humiliation and self-doubt." Such children will be so fearful of making mistakes and receiving censure that they will have difficulty doing things on their own later, when there is no mother figure around to correct them or "do it right" for them. On the other hand, a young child who does exactly as he pleases may grow up to have "an overly extended notion of his own power." She points up the connection between what happens at this phase and later, even adult, feelings of trust, initiative, and self-confidence.

Gifted mothering

Initiative, Erikson's third stage, occurs toward the end of the early years. Just as faith and hope grew from the trust stage, will power grows from autonomy. In initiative, the child uses aggressiveness to express his will and get his way, but seeks to avoid guilt and jealousy toward others. Purpose is the characteristic accomplishment of this stage; in it, the child directs his energies to external activities such as building blocks or learning to count. He's striving to overcome feelings of inferiority or inadequacy through growing competence in doing things.

This autonomy/initiative stage always involves some risks on the part of both mother and child: The mother must be able to let the child take the risks necessary for learning and development. Clearly, this is the period when the groundwork for self-reliance could be laid. Many children have difficulty separating from their parents at this stage because their parents can't separate from them. The mother who can never bear to leave her children, who doesn't know a babysitter she is so sure she'll never need one, who hovers around the nursery school waiting to see if her youngster "might have a problem," is a familiar type to those who work with children. There's powerful evidence that giving children freedom and initiative—taking these all-important risks—can have lasting positive values for achievers.

- *Autonomy and initiative in the survey sample* It's clear that the experts make a profound connection between closeness in the early years and future behavior. It's unlikely, however, that many of the survey mothers recognized or worried about their children's "second birth," not only because these studies weren't published until most of their children were past babyhood, but because most of them, by their own admission, didn't read the experts. One, asked what she'd change if she could do it over again, said she wouldn't read as many books on child rearing! Nevertheless, they seem to have instinctively responded in a way that matched the experts' suggestions when it came to autonomy and initiative, just as they had with closeness and trust:

There is a thin line between being interested in a child and taking over his life, between supporting children and babying them. These mothers clearly knew the difference. While they lavished love and attention on their children, they also made demands upon them—particularly that they do for themselves whatever they could. And we daresay these mothers expected their children to do many things unassisted a bit sooner than other parents might. Indeed, our data revealed that nearly half the mothers expected their children to put away their own things by the age of five—something many parents assume to be beyond children twice that age.

Half expected their children to do homework on their own by the age of six (about the time they started getting it), and two-thirds expected their children to meet this responsibility by the time they were seven. Few regretted having demanded responsibility early. In fact, the mother of a well-known writer told us that if she could raise her son again, she would "try to throw responsibility on him earlier and not make things too easy."

To pursue this further, we tried out a famous theory linking autonomy to achievement on the survey group. David McClelland, the researcher who defined the need to achieve and whose findings on religion and social class we've already discussed, theorized that mothers who stressed independence and success for their sons fostered high need for achievement in the boys. He said, however, that this was only on condition that the mother's interest in having the child make decisions for himself was genuine—not just to make the child less of a burden. Age was also a factor: The child had to be old enough to make decisions but young enough to internalize parental standards of independence and success as his own.

McClelland tested his notion on mothers of boys age 6 to 9, giving them a list of seven items and asking them to choose the two that they found "nicest about little children." These were the items: they listen to what you tell them to do; they're clean and neat; they're polite and well behaved with others; they play nicely with others; they hug and kiss you; they learn to do something after a long time; playtime with mother.

McClelland also tested their sons for the need to achieve. He then put his results together and found that mothers of sons with low need for achievement tended to make their choices from among the first four items, which stress obedience and conformity. Mothers of sons with high need for achievement were more likely to choose from among the last three—the more emotional and involved alternatives.

The survey mothers, who had all raised achievers, affirmed McClelland's results. The great majority made choices from among the last three items, illustrating again their practice of granting autonomy, but in a safe and affectionate environment.

It's fascinating to see how the expert findings supported what the mothers were already doing—and not the other way around. We'll see more examples of how the mothers continued to maintain this early balance between control and encouragement as their children got older.

How stimulation can affect accomplishment

One of the questions posed in this book is how to take the raw material that a child is and help mold it into a young person who is not only intelligent, but able to use that intelligence in his own behalf; in other words, to achieve on his own. The gifted child expresses his native intelligence very effectively, so that the character-building problems become more important than enhancing the brainpower. However, most of us have less-than-gifted youngsters. Can we *make* them into gifted children? It appears we can certainly help.

We've already said that stimulation at a very early age has a lot to do with this, and some amazing research recently underscored this. Allison Clarke-Stewart studied groups of firstborns from low-income black and white families. She first illustrated that contact with the mother was the central component of the child's social experience: infants from nine to thirteen months spent over 80 percent of their waking time in the same room with their mothers. About 20 percent of this was taken up in satisfying physical needs (feeding, changing, bathing, and so on); around 35 percent in physical, social, or verbal interaction with the mothers; and the remaining 45 percent in looking at or playing with materials (toys, objects, TV).

Of the three activities, Clarke-Stewart discovered that the children's intellectual progress related neither to the first, the amount of maternal caretaking, nor to the third, the stimulation inherent in the environment, such as the number or type of toys. Instead, it connected strikingly to the second, that of *maternal responsiveness*. The three aspects of mother's care that best encouraged accomplishment seemed to be verbal stimulation, such as talking or singing to the child; positive attitudes and emotions, such as smiling, hugging, expressing enjoyment, warmth and affection; and social stimulation, such as showing him things and playing with him. The more the mother responded directly to the child in these ways, the faster the child's "information processing" and social, emotional, and language skills developed.

Mediator of the environment is the name Clarke-Stewart gave to this role of the mother in bringing the outside world to the child through the medium of her own

Gifted mothering

personality, words, and actions. Clarke-Stewart found that the white mothers in her group spent more time in this role, talking and playing with their children, whereas black mothers spent more time controlling and physically caring for theirs. The black infants tended to be more physically attached to their mothers than white babies were, and the white youngsters were found to develop intellectual skills sooner and more fully than the black children.

Finally, as one might imagine, maternal rejection was found to lead to negative behavior in children, bearing out the other research we've been discussing. Positive emotion felt and displayed by mothers toward their babies led to enhanced performance by the children in intellectual development and motivation. In general, *maternal responsiveness to the child's social signals enhanced the child's later intellectual and social performance.*

Should you have any lingering doubts that mother can make a difference in raising achievers, at least on the score of providing stimulation, a stunning example of the difference a parent can make to a child's intellectual development is given by Aaron Stern in his book, *The Making of a Genius*.

When his daughter Edith was born, Stern was ill with cancer and unemployed; he was also told the prognosis for Edith's health wasn't good. He developed an intense, unswerving determination to raise Edith to be a genius, employing his own "total submersion" method. He devoted almost all his waking hours to the education of his daughter, following his own theory—that *from birth,* a child is capable of absorbing knowledge. The interests of the child, *not the parent,* direct this process, which becomes integrated into the entire day.

Stern's educational program and Edith's astounding accomplishments included starting her off at three weeks listening to classical music twenty-four hours a day. By four months she was being read to daily and could recognize spoken words; a year or so later she was doing two-digit math and beginning to read. By age five she had read the family's 24-volume encyclopedia, and by fifteen she had finished college and was teaching at university level. It's interesting to note that throughout, and especially at the very early periods, Edith's parents made a point of speaking to her clearly and directly in full sentences, and answering every question thoroughly.

Stern was subjected to ridicule for how he had raised his daughter, but he maintained that she was a happy, sensitive child who was well-adjusted to her unique talents. He has since published and lectured widely on his methods, but perhaps the best support for his claim is this remark from Edith herself: "I don't think that my childhood cramped my emotions or anything like that. When I have children, I plan to raise them in exactly the same fashion."

The fact is that with a great deal of attention and a very early introduction to education, Stern *did* make what we assume was a bright but otherwise ordinary child into an extraordinary achiever. Very few parents can afford to make this kind of investment in time and energy in one youngster, but it certainly shows the results of intense involvement and the importance of impressions made, and time spent, in the early years.

- *Survey mothers as mediators of the environment* It will come as no surprise that the survey mothers were superb mediators of the environment. None of them went to the lengths of Mr. Stern, but one or two actually came close. Nearly 100 percent read to their children when they were small. Most said they started when the children were approaching two, but some began almost at birth. It was interesting to see that mothers of famous artists and authors began reading to their children somewhat sooner than mothers of children from the other groups. All the mothers read to their children often: 88 percent at least a few times a week; 38 percent every single day. The majority continued until the child reached school age; some kept it up much

Gifted mothering

longer. This may well have been as much from the pleasure in the shared experience as from the feeling of value in imparting new information—a conclusion we could easily draw from our knowledge of the mothers' attitudes.

Mediating the environment didn't stop with early childhood. The mothers maintained their commitment to bringing their world to their children; and we see in Chapter 9, which discusses education at home and at school, how important this became when the children grew older.

Even if we didn't have all this evidence of the importance of involvement and stimulation, we certainly have evidence of the disastrous effects of life without it. Physician René Spitz wrote of children who grew up in English institutions where their physical needs were seen to but their mental and emotional ones weren't: No one talked to or played with them. Their development lagged badly and in some cases this led to a condition in which they ceased to grow normally—lack of stimulation simply arrested some forms of development altogether. Spitz termed this condition "hospitalism."

It isn't necessary to live in an institution to suffer from serious understimulation and neglect. Many children living with their families are victims. Every hospital emergency room in the country knows of the high incidence, especially in poor neighborhoods, of small children being injured by playing with matches, darting into traffic, or eating dangerous food or medicine. Their underprivileged parents haven't known to give them even the basic instruction on physical survival which comes almost instinctively to parents who have received it themselves as children.

4. Gifted mothering and the hot coal technique

The third component of gifted mothering, after expectation of greatness and intense involvement, was early recognition and enthusiastic support of the child's gifts and interests. Though most of the mothers were reluctant to claim any credit for their children's accomplishments, many said if they did help at all, their single greatest contribution was in *recognizing the child's talent early and encouraging it.*

Arlo Guthrie's mother believes this is universal with all children: "With any child, my grandchildren, my children, the children I taught over the years, you have to find that essential thing in them, and then you work to bring it out. It's different in each child, but it's always there." Shirley Silverman, mother of opera star Beverly Sills, echoed this in a recent *New York Times* article: "You have to give them a

Gifted mothering and the hot coal technique

dream. Whether it comes true or not, let them have some direction with this dream."

The power of mother's inspiration and encouragement is hard to overstate. Examples of it abounded in the survey sample, and turn up in other stories of how accomplished people got their first inspirations. We've already discussed children of artistic and scientific families, where this obviously played a role. Here's more from the Silverman family. From Beverly: "My mother introduced me to opera. ...my earliest memory is of Mamma cranking up the Victrola every morning and putting on those Galli-Curci records. She has a lovely voice herself. She used to play piano." And from Shirley: "After I fought for a sofa, I got Papa to buy us a piano. I insisted. Then I went to 14th Street and bought all kinds of sheet music and records. When she was only three, I took Beverly to a Lily Pons concert... 'Mamma, someday I want to sing like Lily Pons,' she told me."

This kind of early motivating experience can be the first turning point in raising an achiever. Dr. Phyllis Cohen of Yale, who's been working on musical creativity in children, describes situations very much like the Silvermans, where the parent brings the activity to the child, acts it out, teaches it, and conveys enthusiasm for it years before the child is ready to make it on his own. This creates an informal learning environment, much as a music school provides a formal one through courses and role models (teachers and concert professionals) for older students.

- *The culture-bearer* This function of the mother as the transitional figure bridging the gap between the child's early experimentation and later independent expression of talent bears the same relation to culture as mediator of the environment does to the physical and mental surroundings of the child. In fact, it's been called the role of the culture bearer. Many cultures have recognized this role of the mother. The widely used Suzuki system of instrument instruction, from Japan, has the mother actually learning and playing the violin right along with the child. She thus becomes the primary reinforcement motivating the youngster to learn. Of course, this is nothing new in principle: Parents have always handed down the songs and stories and nonpractical information of their culture to their children right along with how to grow vegetables and catch rainwater. But it is worthwhile to be consciously aware of the effect you can make in this area.

- *Stage mothers* When we learn of heavy maternal involvement in an achiever's background, we often assume mother sacrificed all to her child to satisfy some frustrated ambition of her own. But among our sample, we were surprised to find that Faye Dunaway was right; few of the mothers expressed even a hint of this syndrome. Rather, they gave the impression of being complete personalities in their own right, with a wide range of satisfactions; generally optimistic and pleased with their lives; and remarkably free of frustrations, at least any they would admit to. We discuss the mothers outside their maternal roles in Chapter 8, on role models, but it seemed appropriate to raise the stage-mother matter here where we talk about spotting early talent. Beverly Sill's remark settles the matter: "Whatever our dreams were, Mamma tried to make them come true. But she never pushed me in my career. She was never ambitious or aggressive. Unless I ask for advice, my mother stays out of my professional life."

The hot coal technique

Probably because of their own sense of personal fulfillment, the survey mothers were open-minded about their child's particular talent or gift, letting it unfold naturally, but then encouraging it enthusiastically, as one gets a fire going by blowing on hot coals. Zula Crichton's story of her son Michael's blossoming interest in science is a good example:

Gifted mothering and the hot coal technique

> *When he was around sixth or seventh grade, we all went on a nature hike. It was the first we'd taken that had a printed guide. He was absolutely fascinated, so I said to him, "Michael, you really ought to write this up." Well, he did, and sold it to* The New York Times.... *Earlier, in the fourth grade, the school had a program on electricity, and he came home and wired lights up all over the basement and in his closet. Then they started multi-school science projects. Of course I had to drive him to them, so I sat through every one of them* [emphasis ours]. *Michael wrote a fabulous project and won first prize. Every year after, he would do one. They got more and more scientific. Magazines, like* Colliers, *were doing wonderful issues on space at that time, and he began to correspond with the editors, especially the one at* Scientific American. *They were fabulous to him....*

It is hard to capture or express what it means to any of us when someone suggests that we run for office, write a poem, do a painting, or give a talk. It is a moment of direct inspiration, because it conveys their faith that we have the ability to achieve the objective. When a parent says this type of thing to a child, it can profoundly affect his self-image for years. Sadly, many children grow up feeling they are second-rate, unworthy, unwanted, and incapable; or capable only of certain qualities parents or teachers have assigned to them, such as being funny, or slow, or "good at math but not at art." In this way, youngsters become programmed. How different when a parent can say, "You should write an article or a song, or do whatever it is you want to do, and I feel you will do it well."

Supporting this idea, Dr. Cohen says that "the parents' role is of great importance—in fact, parents can be the critical factor." She is convinced that any outside musical training only reinforces an atmosphere created earlier in the child's home environment, rather than the reverse:

> *It may not be anything specific. Records and concerts are not enough. Children's concerts are often not*

really for children, and records have to be chosen carefully to have a noticeable effect. It is more often the satisfaction the parents convey that they are getting from the child's accomplishment. They may foster independence, but at the same time they must get satisfaction out of what the child does, and believe it's worthwhile. After all, they are sacrificing time, money, energy—so they want to believe it's worthwhile. Kids sense this. The props, like records and books, however costly, may augment the process but they can also get in the way.

In fact, stressed Dr. Cohen, "affective or emotional impoverishment is far more devastating to talent than economic impoverishment....If there is one important message to get across, it would be that one."

- *Supporting interests with outside training* The survey mothers seem to have gotten the message. Not only did they create a secure, loving environment, a sort of "inside training" for the fostering of the child's burgeoning interest or talent, they also supported it heavily with outside lessons. The study reported that most of the parents

    ...*managed to provide some sort of formal training outside school. Music lessons headed the list, but other popular areas were sports (particularly riding and tennis), religion and dance. Even parents with very low incomes made certain their children received special instruction. One mother worked in a cannery, and her husband was a manual laborer, but their son, now a successful artist, nevertheless had violin lessons. In all, nearly 90 percent of the famous offspring got some sort of training to supplement their formal education.*

The leading mother in this category was truly dedicated to her youngster's gift, having provided ear training, theory, piano, violin, ballet, tap, acrobatics, Spanish, German, baton, castanets, typing, shorthand, English, and math. Few could match the intensity of her activity to nourish the extraordinary talents of her child at a very young age, but the commitment to supplemental education and training was almost universal. And this meant finding the teachers, financing the training, and, in most cases, transporting children to and from lessons over the years.

Katharine Fryer, the mother of scientist Sarah Leibowitz, comes from a whole family of artistic and gifted people, including painter Winslow Homer and composer Samuel Barber. She feels that being raised in an atmosphere where talent was encouraged helped her children become achievers, and shared a delightful memory of such encouragement from her own childhood: "I once made a little picture of a rose. I even cheated a little bit on it—I copied a part. Everyone said, 'That's a beautiful rose,' and they rushed me off to a painting teacher. Whatever we did, they were terribly proud. There was no condescension at all."

Mrs. Fryer admits to having some minor artistic skill, but it amuses her to think of the spontaneity and enthusiasm with which art lessons were arranged for the little girl who had cheated a bit. Her humor is an integral part of the understanding that goes with fostering—or even abandoning—dreams of talent. Most of the survey mothers were able to switch gears when talents changed, or to let up when a child's inclination was altered by growing maturity. Unlike stage mothers, they could stand back from their own dreams if the child's interests took a new direction, as often happened.

- *Recognizing the artistic child* Back In Chapter 2 we spoke of the nonprodigy child, saying not to be disturbed if your youngster isn't drawing like Rembrandt at two. But what if he or she is? What do you do? We came across an interesting group studying the creative process in children. They call themselves Project Zero, because there was zero information on the subject when they started. They've suggested that your youngster may go on to be a Rembrandt, or he could wind up a doodler. It's possible you could make the difference.

First, they looked at our natural artistic-growth process, beginning with the time when—as still illiterate children—we hum tuneless tunes or scribble with crayons as soon as they're given to us. Project Zero director Howard Gardner says these are the stages:

During the first year or two of life, the infant comes to know the world directly, through his senses and his action. In the years following infancy, from two to seven, he comes to master the symbols of his culture—language, hand gestures, movement of the body, pictures, figures of clay, numbers, music. By the age of five or six, children understand these symbols and can often combine them in striking ways. Then things change. School-age children are inclined to succumb to convention and follow the rules governing a given activity. Their language becomes conservative and their art may be limited to the copying of forms and representation of the "real world."

We can all certainly remember being rewarded for learning to color inside the lines and duplicate letters and pictures with accuracy. This abandonment of imagination in favor of copying, or literal stage of the creative process, has been disparaged; but Gardner feels that it might be an important or even crucial phase, because it's a mastery of rules that is a necessary precursor to artistic progress in the long run.

After the literal period comes the sensitive period, the years just prior to adolescence. The youngsters, who have now mastered the accepted conventions, become sensitive to the work of others, whether teachers, students, magazine illustrators, or old masters. They also become sensitive to criticism of their own work from themselves as well as others. If the artistic youngster has been able to develop real skill by this time, he'll be more able to withstand his emerging critical sophistication; he can see he's "not so bad" and will continue. If not, he may—as have most of us—put down his clay and paintbrushes forever and

Gifted mothering and the hot coal technique

pass into art appreciation rather than creation. Those who do stay to become artists subsequently create in a way that is fundamentally different from the random and innocent inventions of children. Their creativity is now combined with a full awareness of the rules, and they make conscious rather than naive departures from them into innovation.

Project Zero tested these stages and theories against the life stories of famous artists. In doing so, they discovered that the three following aspects seemed to be required for serious artistic achievement:

(1) *Inborn talent.* This is the natural aptitude which must be there: the ability to sketch skillfully; have an eye for colors; sing in tune; identify rhythms; act; dance; perform; have a feel for words, gestures, intonations.

(2) *Early environment.* This is where parents come in, providing materials and inspiration, such as pencils, paints, records, instruments, and enthusiasm. Basically, Gardner's group feels this may be all that is needed at this preschool stage.

(3) *Active intervention.* This is where teachers join parents, providing instruction and examples, getting the literal stage under way. Gardner's research showed that virtually all creative artists had gone through a literal stage, but evidently rapidly or fluidly enough so that by adolescence they had become more freely creative, and had thus passed through the barrier of the self-conscious sensitive period.

- *The bridge of motivation* Note that inborn talent is only one of the components. The other two show the vital role of parents. Again and again we find that the critical factor in later achievement is the moment when the youngster stops doing whatever it is to please his parents, and starts doing it to please himself. Parents play a vital role in getting the child to this bridge so that he may cross it.

    Dr. Cohen spoke of it as "internalizing the motivation." First she described the musical prodigy—one who has the ability to duplicate rhythms and pitches, to withstand frustration and concentrate for long periods, and who has advanced coordination. Then she described the transitional period when this or any such inborn talent is either pushed forward or left fallow:

> *The crucial [stage] is adolescence. Most students stop in the pre-adolescent period. The teacher and parent have to be very sensitive to pull through this time....It's difficult to anticipate who will internalize the motivation, making it his or her own. This is the passage that must occur for the work to proceed into mastery, if not virtuosity. Parents can support and encourage at this stage, but it is ultimately up to the adolescent to carry on.*

Burt Bacharach's mother, who believed in her son's talent and had for years been the chief proponent of his studying the piano, remembered this transition as being rather a surprise: "He was to be given the chance of discontinuing at age sixteen, but shortly before that, he began to truly enjoy playing, and needed no further urging."

- *Other kinds of achievers* Although the examples given by Dr. Cohen and Project Zero refer to artistic talent, similar stages can relate to all expressions of achieving gifts—whether graphic or performing arts, science, mathematic or verbal ingenuity, or even organizational, managerial, or leadership gifts, though these may seem less obvious in the early years. Not to everyone, however. The mother of a prominent banker distinctly remembered her "continual encouragement that he was a leader," starting when her son was six years old. "I knew then he had ability in this line," she said. The message of the hot coal technique is still the same.

In considering the matter of varying abilities, we were intrigued to learn about a theory that related different types of achievers to the homes that produced them. In a book called *The Productive Personality,* John Gilmore divided productive people—or achievers—into three categories: the scholar, the creator (in art or science), and the leader. He saw each as a different personality type, making a different contribution. He observed, just as our survey data indicated, that for all types of productive people a stable home, relatively conflict-free, seemed a prerequisite. The father tended to be responsible and respected, while the mother was "emotionally secure and supportive." Thereafter, Gilmore concluded that:

The academic achiever, or scholar, had highly educated parents who directed their attention toward education. The mothers were *involved and interested* in their children's developing academic skills.

Creative people came largely from homes where less attention was directed toward living up to parental expectations. These children had more *respect* and *autonomy,* and seemed less intimate with their parents than the other productive types. The child experienced little pressure to conform, and could explore a number of different identities or "selves."

Leaders learned more interpersonal than concrete or academic skills. That is, they learned how to handle people, and get things done through others, rather than pursuing the more private and independent skills of the scholar and artist/scientist. The parent-child relationship was exceptionally warm, and a great deal of *emotional security* was provided by the parents.

We have italicized factors that recur again and again in this research—and which also were the very things stressed by the survey mothers.

Children as top priorities

No matter what type of achiever you may be able or interested to produce, talent is required. But for the gift to bloom, the other stages must also be passed through; and that's where nurturing, closeness, support, encouragement, mediating the environment, culture bearing, and all the other myriad roles of the gifted mother come into play.

Filia Holtzman, mother of twins—her congresswoman daughter was in our sample—provides a good example of the three components of gifted mothering in action: expectations of success, intense involvement, and encouragement of early talent. Her story is particularly inspiring to us today, since she worked much of the time her children were growing up.

At five, both twins had started piano. Mother and father read to the children from infancy, and their father and grandfather took them on numerous excursions, boat rides, and to museums. Mrs. Holtzman emphasized her interest in keeping the children busy, "encouraging them in all areas—whenever I could help them, I tried." A highly organized person, she managed many responsibilities, including teaching college at night, while raising her youngsters. She thinks they were constantly stimulated, surrounded by loving relatives, and that they derived a great deal from their challenging, cultured environment.

Chevy Chase's mother, who admits to "thirty-six years of experience as a mother," says she is "not an organized person," but "the one thing they could count on was my full attention to them. I have always been very protective and my emotional life is closely tied to them." Creative and artistic herself, she was immersed in a musical career when her older children were quite young, practicing four to six hours a day. She gave it up. "When they ran their toy trucks up and down the piano keys, I saw what was going to happen. I knew the world would not be affected by my musical career, but the lives of my sons would be deeply affected by my job as a mother. It was a conscious decision which I never regretted."

Both these mothers were addressing the difficult question of priorities. Elizabeth Holtzman's mother was organized and kept a career going for many of her child-rearing years, but the children were always central. She felt she managed this by having her priorities very clear. The performer's mother, although not as organized, simply put accessibility to her children at the top of the list.

One has the unmistakable sense from all these stories of the solid commitment which comes through regardless of any details of a given family situation. This commitment of the mother to her relationship with her child was established early, so that long before she had to cope with pressures from the outside world—schools, summer camps, parties, allowances, jobs—she had already formed a continuing pattern of giving time, energy, and imagination to her child's future.

5. Mothers and fathers: sharing the commitment and the parenting partnership

Although our study concentrated on mothers, the figures for family stability (84 percent of the families stayed intact during child rearing) make it clear that in most cases Dad was on hand. Moreover, the survey data show that the parents worked very well as child-rearing partners, and that Dad usually played an active role in child rearing himself, as inspiration, peacemaker, and disciplinarian, in addition to being breadwinner.

We're well aware that today's family is very different from that of most of our superachievers: the incidence of nonintact or single-parent homes is far greater. In Chapter 10 we give specific tips on raising achievers in working-mother and single-parent households, but all our research confirms that *the values and attitudes toward family life were consistent throughout the sample, appearing in both two-parent and single-parent homes.* Once again, it's the point of view that matters.

Let's hear it for father

We've already met the moms who, when asked their greatest contribution to their child's success, said they made no contribution; those who said "being there"; and those who said it was blowing on the hot coals of talent early. Now we're going to hear from the last group—those who said it was marrying Dad. One woman said simply, "Marrying my husband and together maintaining a good family home."

- *Confidence in choice of mate* This modest gratitude for good fortune in the choice of a husband was expressed in a number of ways. (These women didn't seem to realize that their husbands had also made fortunate choices!) One mother wrote in glowing terms characteristic of many of the group, "I am a very happy person and have had a delightful life. My husband was a beautifully educated man, also an athlete; he was a delightful companion and father and at meals there was always conversation about world events, etc. As a result, my sons were very well informed...." Dr. Kate Barany put it this way: "I chose a wonderful husband, who was interested and supportive, to raise a close-knit family with morals and dedication."

    Mrs. Crichton described her husband's attitude: "Whatever was important to you was important to him. He had an incredible way of making people bloom. He was always supportive, always had time for us and the children. He traveled a lot, so he would set up the calendar at home so we would know just where he would be and when he would be back. He would bring back a carnation from a dinner because he knew how I loved them, and we'd put it out on the breakfast table. He *always* had time for us."

- *New research on fathers* As the *Family Circle* article says, "Interestingly, the research bias against father, which probably started with Freud's conviction that mother was far more important, is finally breaking down. Scientists are devoting more and more attention to the relationship between the father and his children, sometimes with fascinating results."

    Research by psychologists Ross Parke and Douglas Sawin revealed the unique contribution fathers can make to the care and development of young children. In most families observed, fathers could do caretaking (feeding, changing, and so on) as well as mothers, but because—even in the most liberated homes—mother wound up doing it anyway, fathers spent four to five times as much time playing with their children as they did caretaking. They also played differently: "more physically arousing and unusual activities, for instance, such rough and tumble play as tossing the infant in the air." Mothers, in comparison, were more likely to talk and smile at the babies, use toys or "play conventional games such as peekaboo."

- *Fathers as inspiration* The majority of mothers in the survey felt they had been fortunate in having husbands who were inspirations to their offspring. Many spoke emotionally of the great admiration between father and son. Mrs. Gibson described her husband as a remarkably reliable and consistent man—"He worked thirty years and never missed a day"—and her son Kenneth was "steady and reliable, too." She said that when he took music lessons, his teacher "always told me he would be the one student who would show up for a lesson on a snowy day; he'd be sitting there, and he'd hear Kenneth's big boots clomping down the hall." She believed that "the most dominant influence [on her sons] was the relationship with their father," and said of Kenneth, "I never saw anybody love a father like he loved his father."

Mrs. Bacharach described the relationship between her son, Burt, and his father, columnist and author Bert Bacharach: "They are very similar. Burt has a certain humility; my husband is very much the same way, rather an unusual man. I think their appeal is based on that humility that comes through..."

Atlanta mayor Maynard Jackson's mother wrote that "the image of a successful, eloquent father in the pulpit every Sunday" was a crucial influence on her son's later achievement.

Many of the fathers were specific influences on their children's talents and ultimate success; artistic gifts, such as those shared by Andrew Wyeth and his son, Jamie, represent that unique situation in which a child can imitate his parent at the same time he is being helped to develop his own talent and career—an apprenticeship within the parent-child relationship.

Other fathers contributed by making a heavy involvement in time and attention, even at the end of their own long working day. Connecticut State Senate majority leader Joe Lieberman said:

Dad always held us to high standards—for example, to do well in school. Doing average was never good enough. He was always actively involved in our education. I wasn't especially good in math, and I remember him spending time with me in the critical moments, learning new concepts and going over them again and again; he was tough. But every act of achievement was rewarded in our family...."

- *Emotional reactions to father* Stories, poems, paintings, even pieces of music dedicated to, drawn from, caricaturing, and praising fathers have been produced by their offspring since time began. Of course there are as many or probably more for mothers, but children's feelings about fathers have an entirely different quality. Perhaps because fathers are usually away at work, remote champions doing mysterious things in the family's cause, there is often a desire to impress, be more adult, be or do something that "father can be proud of." Feelings of gratitude are more commonly expressed for mom, who was, as we know, "always there."

We're talking about that mixed bag of feelings we all have toward Dad. A most eloquent expression of it comes from novelist John Updike, who writes often about such emotional corners of life. He was profiled recently in *The New York Times* by journalist James Atlas, who described how Updike's father had lost his job during the Depression, and his grandfather had had to go to work as a road repairman. Things had worsened until the family—Updike, his parents, and maternal grandparents—had finally moved back to their "picturesque but primitive" farmhouse in Pennsylvania which lacked even running water. Updike's father got a teaching job and they all lived on his salary of less than $1,800 a year.

The Centaur, Updike's 1963 novel may be, as Atlas asserts, "a portrait of the adolescent Updike's troubled relationship with his father, an ineffectual high-school math teacher." But the description of this figure in the novel is so sensitive and empathetic that it is almost painfully touching:

Understand that to me, my father seemed changeless. In fact, he did look younger than his years. When he turned his head toward me, his face was that of a sly street urchin prematurely toughened. He had been a child in a humble neighborhood of Passaic. His face, compounded of shiny lumps and sallow, slack folds, to me seemed both tender and brutal, wise and unseeing; it was still dignified by the great distance that in the beginning had lifted it halfway to the sky. Once I had stood beside his knees on the brick walk leading to the grape arbor of our house in Olinger and felt him look level into the tops of the horse-chestnut trees and believed that nothing could ever go wrong as long as we stood so...."

Here Updike has captured what every child experiences in the protective shadow of his father. In the survey sample, examples of powerful paternal influence appeared in every area, from education and ideals to hobbies and careers.

Sharing the profoundest commitment

Probably the most resounding parental impact of all can be seen in the degree to which parents supported their children's gifts and hopes, emotionally as well as practically. We've spoken of the potent combination of mother's commitment in the form of expectations, involvement, and support. When you add father's to that, the effect is more than redoubled.

Accomplished people often surprised their parents by displaying unusual absorption or determination as children. What does a parent make of the extraordinary capabilities of a Twyla Tharp? Or the decisiveness of four-year-old Yves St. Laurent telling his aunt what to wear? The key is what you do with it. The survey parents seemed to understand that such children, as all others, need continuing support from their parents, *especially when they can't get it anywhere else.*

Otherwise this gift—which *is* a gift, but which can also be the source of unhappy "strangeness" as it separates the achiever from his peers—may be pushed aside to protect the developing social ego. The critical achievement of the survey parents was their ability to nurture the gift within the child while also nurturing the child. An accomplished entertainer's mother expressed this perfectly when she wrote that her most important contribution had been "encouraging him to be whatever he felt he was, despite judgments of others—teachers, neighbors, etc."

A compelling example of what this kind of support can mean to an achiever appeared in a recent magazine article on bright children. It described a little girl from a large family of high-I.Q. youngsters. Like Edith Stern, she had been tutored from babyhood by her father and had arrived at kindergarten already able to read and write; her schoolmates were just starting their ABCs. She endured years of being labeled a "brain" by fellow students and being passed over by teachers who wouldn't call on her. The ultimate blow came when she was heading for college and had won more than a dozen scholarships: "The principal told her that winners were no better than anyone else, just luckier."

How did this exceptionally bright youngster manage these slings and arrows and stay true to her early promise? "I got through because my father kept telling me I was great....That was all the strength I needed to face setbacks, like teachers who hated me."

This little story also confirms other aspects of our research: the positive influence fathers can have on daughters; intense involvement—in this case almost from birth; and encouragement of initiative. But most of all, it shows the incredible power of unshakable parental support in the face of resistance.

The famous long-range Terman study actually documented this in its research. About twenty years after the study started, and again twenty years after that, the researchers reviewed the data and sorted out the most successful men from the least successful, seeking clues to what made for achievement—or lack of it—in a group which had started in the same place at the same time with roughly the same intellectual equipment. They found many variables among family backgrounds, but one of the widest gaps between the two groups was the amount of encouragement parents gave for initiative and independent behavior: the successful group reported much more encouragement from both parents.

Hand in hand with the emotional support went the technical commitment these parents freely made with outside lessons, time, money, transportation. Father's contribution was abundantly expressed in the survey sample: Twyla Tharp's mother described her husband as "magnificent in his interest and cooperation." Belle Kirschner remembered her husband's taking the youthful Don to an amusement park just so he could cut little records for twenty-five cents.

The survey parents seemed to agree on giving their children permission to be what they could; not to push, but to promote the child's gifts and interests, even as they changed and new ones emerged. Sometimes they seemed to come out of nowhere:

> *Neither my husband nor I are very musically inclined and we were rather surprised when our son asked to take piano lessons when he was in the 6th grade. We bought a piano… and told him we would pay for lessons as long as he practiced without having to be nagged about it. He took classical lessons for five years, twice a week, and practiced every morning before school with no prodding from us. Then the era of guitars came in and he quit and took a few guitar lessons, and from then on he seemed to have no interest in the piano. He started composing small songs about current interests in about the 8th grade, and went on, getting really into it in college, but took no music courses.*

This is a perfect picture of the independently motivated youngster many mothers dream about, but it's an even better picture of supportive parents. This mother had provided all kinds of early stimulation for her son—including riding, golf, and other lessons, none of it musical. In fact, she worried that she'd pushed too hard. But when the boy showed *his* interest, she and her husband gave it their immediate and continued support. He is now a popular music superstar.

- *Growing up without the commitment* Not every achiever is so lucky. Researchers have now identified what they call super-kids—those children who can live in circumstances of desperate poverty or with alcoholic or abusive parents, and still manage to become not only "all right," but remarkable in some cases. They display the behavior of gifted children—intense absorption, autonomy, initiative, and creativity or scholarship or leadership (or all three).

Whatever their achievements, chances are they'll all remember having to grow up without the precious advantage of that parental commitment. We spoke to some achievers from less desperate backgrounds who remembered this feeling clearly. They spoke of unhappy childhoods that had driven them to turn to work, creativity, or intellectual achievement to fill the emotional void. They cited the pain of being loners, rejection by peers in adolescence for being too bright or strange, or even rejection by parents for almost the same reasons. Colleen McCullough, author of *The Thorn Birds*, put it this way: "The family was totally anti-intellectual; they rather despised intellect....Father was a running champion. I was fat and read a lot."

The message is clear: You can take Ms. McCullough's view that "opposition is always a tremendous help in furthering pursuits," and wait for your achievers to develop in spite of you. Or you can take a cue from the survey parents and give your children plenty of open support so that any pain they feel from being "too bright or too strange" will be more than counterbalanced by the warm support they receive at home for being *exactly who they are:* your children.

The parenting partnership

Besides sharing a profound commitment to their youngsters, in smoothly working households the parents combine efforts to create a unique parenting style. Their strengths and weaknesses complement each other. If he is poor at figures, she may manage the bills and the budget. If she tends to be impatient, he may be the one who does the best job of listening to the child.

At their best, partners in these marriages reinforce family goals and values in almost everything they do—in beliefs; religious commitment or philosophy of life; behavior toward relatives, friends, and neighbors. This successful intermeshing can be contrasted with those parents who have difficulty communicating, fail to agree on the guiding principles of their lives, and thus get into continual power struggles over the daily details of family life.

- *Agreement on the basics, especially discipline* Many respondents stressed the importance of agreeing on the fundamentals and mutually supporting the whole life-style. Dr. Barany said, "I read many books about education, and discussed this with my husband well in advance. We agreed in all basic principles."

    Mrs. Filer spoke of parental solidarity in one of the trickiest areas of child rearing: discipline. "I think you should *never* say, 'Wait 'til Daddy comes home.' This is the worst thing I ever heard. We always agreed, although I was the chief disciplinarian. This mutual support was very important." Many mothers concurred. Mrs. Crichton gave this example:

    We had a foreign student staying here once. She was going to go off somewhere for the night with a group of kids, and I explained to her that she should not do that, that we would pick her up at the end of the evening and bring her back here. Well, later, when my husband came home, she went over to him and asked him all the same questions all over again. One by one he gave exactly the same answers. She was amazed. What she didn't understand was that we agreed *on every detail; we had discussed all these things again and again and had the same position. Perhaps because she was not an American, she failed to realize the extent to which a mother serves as both parents when her husband must travel a lot for his work.*

- *Sharing time* Most of our achievers were raised before the TV era. This means not only that it wasn't there to seduce the children, it wasn't there to tempt parents either. Radio was, but it was never as compelling. Even if the survey parents weren't really as conscientious as they seemed to be, chances are they talked things over more, just because there was more time to do it. Who could have imagined that today, as sociologist Ray Birdwhistell tells us, married couples tend to talk about twenty-seven minutes a week! We certainly could benefit from increasing this, for if there is no communication, there cannot be much agreement.

Most of the survey fathers seemed able—and willing—to spend time at home. Those who had to travel were described as available emotionally when they *were* home. Just as we dispensed with the stage mother, we'd better clear away the stereotype of the workaholic husband, who plays golf when he isn't at the office and leaves the family pretty much on its own. The survey fathers were visible presences in the family system.

- *Sharing interests* We offered the survey mothers a list of ten activities and interests and asked them to indicate those which appealed to them and their husbands while the child was growing up. There was no limit—they could check as many as they wanted. The most frequently checked item on the list was "Family (spent time with spouse and children; concerned with children's activities in school, etc.)," with almost all the mothers checking it as an activity that appealed to them. Many checked it for fathers too. This reflected another trend: Interest varied greatly from family to family, but within families, better than half the couples shared the same interests, often pursuing them together. Kenneth Gibson's parents, for instance, managed to find time to run for—and win—political office together, becoming local codistrict leaders. Omitting the Family category, and Business, which was checked off for about 60% of the fathers (and 20% of the mothers, interestingly), the chart shows the results. Note the parallel groupings.

Interests Appealing to Parents

	Mothers		Fathers
Music, Arts	82%	Sports	72%
Social	75%	Social	65%
Sports	47%	Music, Arts	58%
Politics	47%	Politics	56%
Crafts	33%	Scientific	39%
Education	31%	Crafts	34%
Scientific	26%	Education	32%

Plus: Community service, religious groups, boards of directors, school boards, travel, and about two dozen other interests.

We also found similarities when we asked the mothers to select which of these interests was most *important* to them and their husbands. Family easily took first place for both parents. These are the rankings:

Interests Most Important to Parents

Mothers	Fathers	
1	1	Family
2	2	Music, Arts
3	5	Social
4	4	Sports
5	6	Politics
6	7	Crafts
7	8	Education
8	9	Scientific
9	3	Business
10	10	Miscellaneous

Using the blank questionnaire at the end of this book, you might consider testing yourself and seeing where you and your spouse stand. The basic categories of interest haven't changed that much. Don't be surprised if you find there's a change in your rankings, however. Recently, in research on women in midlife, Cynthia Pincus asked a group seeking counseling on career changes to rank their priorities. While priorities aren't the same as interests, the list is close enough to give a comparative picture of the survey mothers and these contemporary women. They are described as transitional because they are neither traditional nor feminist, but somewhere in between, like most women today.

Value rankings of "transitional" women

1. Identity—self: activities and goals, "exploring new parts of myself, developing a fuller sense of my own identity"
2. Children: having children, reserving time for them, having a meaningful relationship with them
3. Career: competence, qualifications, improving skills
4. Intellectual, cultural: activities and awareness
5. Marriage, companionship
6. Friendship, overcoming isolation
7. Reentering work or study
8. Financial activities: investments, business, salary considerations
9. Moving up in career
10. Finding an activity that is challenging; making a contribution to the community through service; and maintaining a home environment (all received equal ratings)
11. Devoting time to religious observance; and having a satisfying avocation (received equal ratings)
12. Developing a number of interests; and maintaining close ties with relatives (received equal ratings)

Quite a difference from the *Family Circle* group! Note that "children" and "marriage," the only categories comparable to the "family" in our survey, have sunk to second and fifth places on the list. Career was in between, and "exploring new parts of myself" was at the top. These women were seeking advice and not giving it; nevertheless, this is still a compelling comparison. The little girl who had been taught in the fifties and sixties to yearn for a good marriage and children found that by the time she was ready for them, she was also expected to use her education in visible ways outside the home. The Women's Movement grew from the desire to give women more options in life, but many women felt they had lost some options as well, such as the right to feel comfortable and accepted in traditional domestic roles. This is a difficult transition affecting everyone—men, women and children alike—as social roles are now evolving so rapidly.

- *Enjoyment of differences* One thing that was apparent from the survey was that within the structure of marriage and family life there seemed to be room—and respect—for differences of opinion, taste, and interest. Also, knowing that we change over the years, it was acknowledged that shared interests may hold for some periods but not others. Recognizing the same process of ongoing change in themselves as in their children, the survey parents were able to keep bringing new stimuli and ideas into the home while maintaining flexibility in the basic agreements in order to keep the sensitive balance intact.

- *Sharing child care* As social change accelerates, sharing of domestic roles becomes more and more common. In the families of our respondents, however, only one woman said that her husband had helped with the child care. The majority used relatives, babysitters, and friends or housekeepers if they used paid help. Research studies indicate this was also true of the general population at the time. Fathers are now responding more to the situation by helping out at home, but it's still a slow process. A noted study done not long ago revealed that working wives received *less* help from their spouses than those at home full-time, and that the average working woman put in sixty-six hours a week at her two jobs—the one "at work" and the one at home.

- *Problem solving* In most of these households, problems called for parental conferences, and conferences led to action. This was a joint attack against the evils that can threaten a childhood, always having the welfare of the child as the objective. The Gibsons, told that Kenneth would die because he'd swallowed a toy that couldn't be removed, were advised to prepare for a funeral. Quickly they scraped together the funds to go North and get another opinion, thus saving their son's life.

   One of Katherine Fryer's daughters was virtually wasting away; she was told the treatment was "just very slow." Impatient and courageous, she took the girl to Florida for a change of scene and climate, and worked up her own treatment. Her husband ran their Westchester home and looked after their other four children, giving her the support she needed. Their ailing child began to recover, and Katherine Fryer became a pioneer in the then-almost-unknown affliction of anorexia nervosa.

   A number of parents battled poverty while trying to raise their children as decent, honest people with high ideals. It took the mutual efforts of two hardworking people committed to scrimping and saving to chart the way upward.

   As the children got older, the joint parental attack on problems grew into the family "problem-solving alliance," where all family members together confronted conflicts arising from within and without the family system. We describe this in the following chapter.

- *Special problems of minorities* Black families faced the special challenge of racism in an era lacking the basic human rights we now take for granted. The mother of a distinguished political figure, whose husband was a leading educator and who held an advanced degree herself, felt the major problem she encountered was "trying to rationalize about discrimination or explain it to the children." Andrew

Young's mother, wife of a dentist, said, "He grew up in a southern town with great segregation laws, and it was difficult for us to make him realize that he was an important human being, despite the restrictions of his native New Orleans. We lived in an almost exclusively white neighborhood, and while the boys played harmoniously around home, they were not permitted to participate in recreation facilities that playmates enjoyed...." How did they handle it? "Letting him know that we loved him dearly and were interested in his welfare and his life's work, and that he was an important person."

Maynard Jackson's parents also "worked hard to circumvent the disastrous effects of racism and segregation on the developing ego of a discerning child...." These parents raised six children, whose number now includes not only the mayor of Atlanta, but also a PhD candidate in urban development, two French teachers, a director of teacher training, and a social-work projects director. Clearly, they did a great deal right and their sensitivity to the needs of each child in this large family was a shared concern: "I agreed with my husband that this male child, by his position in the family between the two older and two younger sisters, might need more special attention away from them. This my husband often [gave him.]"

Even where racism was not a problem, parents shared the goal of fighting to get away from ordinariness, to carry out shared goals, to pursue ideals. And to project, for their families, optimism and faith while facing every reality—a difficult feat, as every parent knows.

Comparing parenting partnerships then and now

The dominant impression coming through these accounts is one of idealistic, committed people who approached their jobs as parents with a great deal of thought and care. This is what we should all strive for, and it has nothing to do with social class or income. Parents who are emotionally involved in the carrying out of daily life build strong families, and point up the problems of those who practice avoidance or escape, which can plunge a family into difficulty. Everyone condemns using alcohol or drugs to escape from pressures; unrecognized but much more common is the subtle technique of avoidance when things get rough. Work, socializing, continual busyness, addiction to television, or compulsive housekeeping are all socially acceptable, but take away valuable time and commitment from growing children who need it more.

Any partnership, especially one in transition, works best when there is a solid agreement about roles. For instance, that father is breadwinner and mother concentrates on home and children (whether or not she works), or that mother's and father's careers are of equal importance, so that responsibilities and incomes are shared to support the home situation.

In each case the basic questions will be, Do the husband and wife communicate their feelings, and is there an agreement about the way roles interweave? Do "father" and "mother" mean the same thing to each partner? Can each adapt to the changes within the other?

Meeting these issues is more of a challenge than ever for today's parents. With millions of women entering the work force in serious career capacities for the first time, changes in the partnership rules are inevitable. Whatever the arrangement chosen, whether in single- or two-parent homes, the survey results indicate that taking an involved and supportive parenting stance is more important to raising an achiever than the mere sustaining of a partnership itself.

6. The family life that fosters achievement

Parents and children together create a new collective identity. It's the family, and it's our first and most critical set of relationships, shaping almost everything we think and do for the rest of our lives.

Our survey sample consisted of practically every kind of family—large ones, small ones, studious ones, noisy ones, rich ones, poor ones, middle-of-the-road ones.

But having a family technically, or a place to hang your hat, isn't the same as sharing a warm, safe home. Our research showed that most of our achievers came from such homes. How do some fathers, mothers, and children work so well as families? For answers we looked not only to the survey mothers, but to experts and some achievers themselves.

Many factors are involved in creating a family environment that fosters achievers: parents' attitudes toward each other, toward their children, and in turn, how the children feel about the parents: harmony or disharmony in the household; moral values and principles shared by the parents and instilled in the children; closeness and communication among family members; amount and manner of time spent together; and solving problems as a family.

By far the most important influence shaping family life is simply the way the parents behaved—it is almost impossible to hide things from children in the intimacy of a family; and by setting positive or negative examples, parents present their children with lasting images of what to do—or not to do—as adults.

Becoming aware of family atmosphere

The first clue about how a family operates is the atmosphere it creates. Every family has one. You can sense it immediately on a visit to the home, or even in spending time with members. Clues are direct—a tangle of trikes out front tells you this family is very different from the one next door with the perfectly manicured lawn. Or indirect—do the children seem submissive or rambunctious, talkative or silent, out of control or under control? Under too much control? Do the parents act overburdened or delighted by their youngsters? How do members treat each other? Are they at ease, tense, jocular, hostile?

Almost everything that goes on in a family contributes to its atmosphere, and is reflected back in it. If a family's had a long siege of hardships, but has kept its spirit, the atmosphere may be even more resoundingly positive than in families where nothing much has been going on. In families where the parents don't respect each other, clouds of gloom will hang over the place, no matter how well off they may be in other ways.

Becoming aware of family atmosphere is important for two reasons. First, to identify that feeling we retain in later years, when we've forgotten isolated incidents of family life. The atmosphere you create in the home is what your children will remember as they mature, rather than the day you broke the lawn mower or the day they flunked math (though they'll probably remember those, too). Second, because once you're aware of family atmosphere, you can pay more attention to enhancing it.

The tiniest baby arriving home from the hospital begins to pick up this atmosphere, from the love, tension, joy, and exhaustion that pass through the family, transmitted via his parents' voices, the way they pick up, hold, and feed him. Children of all ages experience these emotional tones keenly, and they are critical to a youngster's growth since his first and sharpest image of himself is the one reflected by his family.

In homes where the tone is optimistic and positive, children tend to feel confident about themselves and their futures. Where the opposite is true, the children tend to blame themselves, unable to believe that their all-knowing, all-powerful parents could be the reason those chilling breezes are blowing through the household.

Though our achievers came chiefly from families with a positive family atmosphere, we know that negative environments can be powerful motivators too. However, achievers from such backgrounds are always looking over their shoulders to be sure they've outdistanced their unhappy home lives, or "shown *them*," whereas achievers from positive homes are achieving to please themselves —they already know the family is behind them no matter what they do.

Domestic harmony or turbulence? The mothers respond

We approached the question of family atmosphere in various ways. The first indicator was family solidarity, exemplified by the simple fact that most of the families stayed intact, the parents married to each other during the child-rearing years.

We then asked the mothers whether family life had been extremely turbulent and emotional, somewhat turbulent and emotional, somewhat calm and harmonious, or extremely calm and harmonious. Most said "somewhat calm and harmonious," but a surprising number—almost 20 percent—said extremely so. Only about 25 percent said family life was somewhat turbulent and emotional, and none went so far as to say disharmony was extreme. These responses were supported by comments such as "Our house belonged to the children. We were noisy, bustling, cheerful and full of music," from Maynard Jackson's mother. Or, "We all seemed to enjoy each other," from Daniel Callahan's.

We also asked them to rate how happy *they* had been when their youngsters were growing up, to see if there were any secret martyrs in the group. Given the choice of extremely content, content, discontent, extremely discontent, only one mother admitted to the latter. The majority said content, and of these fully a third said they were extremely content. This is a picture so rosy that one might infer these women were just making the best of the only real role open to them in those preliberated days. Lest we make such assumptions, one mother wrote, "I know my answers may lead you to believe that there have been no problems. However, I must say that we had great pleasure in our family life. My husband I have often said that we would like to have the entire experience all over again." The mothers we met in a series of personal interviews displayed enthusiasm that was unmistakably genuine.

It would be hard to make excuses or find reasons why these women enjoyed mothering and family life and handled it so well—even those who had to do it alone. They simply did. And, though "family" may have been the priority, it was never allowed to become the kind of obsession that could crush the members. On the contrary, mothering was by no means the only role these women played. We know they spent a good deal of time outside the home, working or involved in other activities. This outside involvement was doubtless a factor in contributing to the harmony of their homes, because it kept these active, talented women from feeling trapped. Whatever the circumstances, the evidence was convincing that what they gave to their families, they gave willingly, responsibly, and with pleasure.

Problems among the survey children— another clue

In preparing the article for *Family Circle*, we knew that children's problems are a major concern to parents, especially those who are involved enough to want to raise achievers. They can also be an indicator of what's going on at home. This is what we found:

> *Asking about children's problems was a more subtle way of looking for family contention. Unhappy or stressed children often develop problems such as bedwetting, nightmares, speech difficulties, learning disorders, vague fears or phobias, or become rebellious and difficult to handle.*
> *Again, only the mothers of famous entertainers reported any prevalence of such problems. Half of these mothers indicated that their children had three or more of these problems. In the other career groups, only one or two children showed as many signs of stress.*
> *Similarly, when we asked how the children got along at school—were there conflicts with teachers or classmates, learning or disciplinary problems, a general dislike for school?—we found that more than three-fourths of the children were free from such troubles. But once again the Entertainment group proved atypical: half of them* did *have problems in school.*
> *This pattern also showed up when we posed the question: "What was the major problem you encountered in raising your son or daughter?" Most mothers answered*

simply, "None." Michael Crichton's mother wrote modestly, "The problems were mine, not his." But there were a number of complaints among the mothers of entertainers. Several mothers reported that their children became rebellious both at home and at school; one remembered seeking outside counseling to help solve the problem. An affluent mother complained of her son's poor disposition and of a tendency to be unappreciative of "the somewhat golden life he lived..."

But most of our successful men and women did not show signs of emotional stress. Further evidence that these children were reasonably well adjusted comes from the fact they almost all got along with their peers. Nearly two-thirds of the mothers said that their children had many friends, and only three mothers described their children as having one close friend or being a loner. Those in the Arts and Letters category may have been less gregarious than the others; two of the three children who had few friends were in this group. Children who later went into business or politics were somewhat more gregarious than the others.

Choosing togetherness: staying close as we get older

We've already discussed the importance of early closeness and trust in getting a child started on the road to achievement. This stage of closeness seemed to have occurred in most of our survey families, bulwarked by an abiding and tolerant love which yet demanded results and striving for attainment. It characterized the early relations between youngsters and their parents.

The second stage of closeness is expressed by the often-heard, "They're a very close-knit family." This usually means that as teenagers and adults, the members spend time with each other as a matter of choice, not just because they're all under the same roof. They enjoy each other. The survey group showed this too: Rosalyn Yalow calls her mother daily; Don Kirschner's says he's "devoted to the family, constantly checking to see what he can do for us." Examples for this kind of family feeling were often set by survey parents and *their* mothers. Kenneth Gibson's mother said of her two sons, "They knew our mothers and how we respected them—the love we gave them, and how they gave it back....Love was all we had to give, but we gave them all we had, and the children knew this, they saw it."

Michael Crichton's mother spoke of it too: "We were never much interested in what they were going to be—we were too busy with what they were doing *now.* The whole family was very close. Both grandmothers were very much involved. He [Michael] had three adults around much of the time; one grandmother was with us evenings and weekends for a number of years. The family remained close....When one would go away to school, the closeness would change, but it would continue."

Many of our survey families made a point of seeing each other often, sometimes traveling long distances for these reunions. Like the rest of us, they giggle over family myths, rituals, jokes, horror stories, even skeletons. A favorite was the Barany family's system of "raisin accounting." This grew out of the fact that they loved raisins on their breakfast cereal. "Eventually we lost raisins for failing to do something, or won them, and we learned about negative numbers that way without even knowing what they were called." An appropriate memory for a family of scientific achievers.

How closeness and harmony can help achievers

This repeated evidence of closeness in the families of achievers does not mean that enforced family closeness, satirized by the term "togetherness," will produce college presidents and movie stars. Closeness is really an outward and visible sign of more important things going on in the family that are inward and invisible. It's a way of saying, "Hey, we're great! We like each other. I like my mother, my dad, my little brother, my big sister. I like me." When every member of the family is unconsciously saying this to himself, then "Why don't you come over for dinner?" or "Why don't we all go Disneyland?" is just an added corollary. A little later on, "Why don't I run for class president?" or "Why don't I apply for that scholarship?" just seem to be down the same track.

This positive attitude also showed itself in natural, open feelings of sharing and giving. One mother said, "In our big family, we have always been very close—they [the children] have always spent time together, and helped each other out. We always emphasized sharing everything: experiences, time, clothes, and money." She felt her illustrious offspring (she has several) had greatly benefited from this "feeling for people and their problems which they've always had."

- *What about harmony at your house?* If your family is distinctly unharmonious and your heart's set on raising true achievers—not children who are performing to satisfy you or get your attention—don't be discouraged. Often we tend to think these disharmonies are something we're stuck with, but they're not. Even in the best of homes, as one mother put it, "If you don't keep working on your relationships, they don't keep going!"

Time is your first ally. If you can make a commitment to change, and start spending some time analyzing problems and working on your relationships, you'll be surprised at the potential for change in your family. You can make the effort on your own or with outside help; either way, the expenditure of your time is well worth it, and can certainly pay off for your children.

It helps to remember that many parents able to provide happy, stable home lives for their children were fortunate enough to grow up in such homes themselves. They are simply duplicating their own parents' example unconsciously. Most of the survey families seem to have been thus blessed, as the remarks of Mrs. Gibson, Mrs. Crichton, and many others attest. Those of us with less-than-ideal examples to follow have to make an extra effort, not only to create a new, positive environment in our homes, but to avoid unconsciously repeating the negative one we inherited. However, many parents have done this brilliantly, so if your example was negative, take courage; there's always plenty of opportunity for growth and change in following better ones.

The things we do "as a family"

More evidence of how families operate can be found merely by looking at things they do as a family: share meals, leisure time, entertainment, vacations. The rest of the time Dad's at work, the kids are in school, Mom's shopping or doing something else on her own.

- *Sharing meals* Family dinners are famous in the memories of many of us, for that's when the secrets came out, accolades and reprimands were administered, everyone's news of the day was shared, and Dad's presence was felt. The dinner table is where many children get their clearest picture of how grown-ups act. When the discussion is of a family problem, a school crisis, a local scandal that's on everyone's lips, the children learn the parents' values by hearing their explanations and criticisms of what went wrong. Depending on the parents' outlook, this involvement can extend to every topic—cultural events, box scores, world politics, how best to arrange the vegetable garden this spring.

The family that eats together is getting much more than nourishment, and the children are learning more than table manners. Many families today, especially when both parents work, are tempted to slap down a cold cut or two in front of the TV. It's a loss of precious time where much of lasting value can be given and gained by family members. Many of the survey mothers stressed this. Filia Holtzman said, "The intellectual atmosphere of the home, frequent discussions at the dinner table of world events, books, music, art" had contributed to her achievers' success.

- *Entertaining* Nor were the survey children banished when guests came. These families—even the less well-off ones—entertained an amazing average of once a week! There was an almost continuous flow of outsiders through the household, and many mothers spoke of bright and interesting dinner guests who woke the children to new ideas. These parents invited and expected their children to share in their world of information, stimulation, and imagination.

- *Sharing the house* Many mothers spoke of "open house" pretty much all the time. Marjorie Guthrie remembered hers as "full of people, sitting on the floor and playing with the children." Rosalyn Yalow's mother said, "My house was always open and she could have her friends in."

- *Sharing vacations* Although a good many parents could have afforded summer camps or housekeepers to take care of children while they were away, almost all of them took the children with them on vacations. Rosalyn Yalow's mother: "The children never went to camp. When we could, we went to the country where they were busy swimming, reading, and seeing their friends."

One of the Barany boys put it this way: "There was a feeling about home; it was not a place you had to get away from. Life was at home. Parents did not go out at night as is the case today; they ate there, had company in." In turn, "We preferred to vacation with the family."

Attitudes toward children

- *Favorites* Feelings toward children seemed equal in most homes. Asked if they had a favorite child, the majority of mothers objected to the question and insisted they had none. One mother said she found the question "unacceptable." All but eleven mothers insisted there had been no favorites, or just didn't answer. Of those who claimed a favorite, nearly all split, with the father favoring one child, the mother another. In several cases, the "star" child was not the favorite.

  Asked which parent the child was most similar to, fathers and mothers came out with almost even scores. But when asked whom the child was closer to, 33 percent of the mothers felt the child was closer to them, 67 percent said equally close to both parents. No mother believed the child was closer to the father than to her.

- *Siblings* There can be few parents with more than one child who don't already know more about sibling rivalries than they wish they did. One of the survey mothers said her biggest problem in raising her achiever was "keeping the peace among the three boys." The mother seemed keenly aware that sibling competitiveness was a double-edged sword: It could stimulate a child to do his best, but could also be the basis of lasting jealousies. Several felt their firstborns had been successful partly because they had "no one ahead of [them] to try to keep up with." Another said her achiever "was always striving to keep ahead of the others, and still is, but being her little sister was not easy, I'm sure. Every success the young one had, teachers were apt to say,

'Oh yes, of course, you know she's the sister of....'" On the other hand, ballerina Suzanne Farrell's mother believed that "having talented older sisters to look up to" had contributed to her daughter's success. She went on to say, "When one speaks of success, I believe the word 'success' should be qualified. I consider my other daughters successful too—though they are not famous."

Many mothers echoed this feeling. Such families often had two, three, or more achievers setting the pace for each other every step of the way. Sarah Leibowitz's mother spoke of the impact of her achieving daughters on each other. They not only inspired and taught one another, they forged a mutual support system against humdrum surroundings. "They just weren't interested in the so-called normal life—football games and the chocolate shop. They would go off to Juilliard and play quartets—they were awfully proud of each other."

These powerhouse women grew up to be concert musicians, a music professor, and a prominent scientist—the achiever from our survey group. She switched from music to science in college. George Plimpton's three siblings are a landscape architect, lawyer, and artist; and Joel Cohen's became a teacher, educational administrator, and attorney. Carol Tucker Foreman, Assistant Secretary of Agriculture, was named an outstanding young woman in America by one civic group, her lawyer brother an outstanding young man by another.

Amost 75 percent of our non-only-children achievers were cited by their mothers as having a close relationship with another sibling. Older brothers tended to tie up with younger brothers and vice versa, and the same was true with girls, suggesting—as Suzanne Farrell's mother remembered—a strong mentoring relationship between older and younger siblings of the same sex. Even when there were only two children in the family, sibling closeness was often indicated regardless of sex.

- *Giving your children the gift of each other* Probably most of the survey mothers made an effort not to show favoritism, an effort that brought results in later years as it enabled the children, feeling equally loved, to be closer to each other. It's much easier to feel friendly toward your siblings if you're not harboring jealousy and the resentment which can last for years, if not a lifetime, that "mother always loved *you* best."

  Children recognize this and they appreciate it. Kate Barany, one mother who acknowledged reading the experts, did this with her two boys, born only a few years apart. The brothers give their mother specific credit for "individualizing" her children. Said one: "She spent time alone with each of us every single day in order to know what was going on in our world. Even the educational toys she bought were carefully chosen to fit our interests, which were *not* the same." The two boys now share an apartment and easy camaraderie, which was founded in the security their mother gave them about themselves as individuals.

- *Acceptance of differences* Just as it was between parents, tolerance—even enjoyment—of differences between children was fundamental to creating this emotional security. "Sarah was a tomboy—that was fine with me." "Kenneth was like a little old man, always thinking." Parents often compare their youngsters negatively to each other and to neighbor children, and can be even more distraught than the children are if they are "different." As we know, this was not the case with these parents. If their youngster could make a good case for what he wanted to do, fine. Never mind what other kids in the family or the neighborhood said. Remember that over 80 percent of survey homes had more than one child—the others grew up too, all different from each other, with their differences respected.

- *When a parent is famous* When parents are competent and admirable, children are often inspired to imitate them, choosing similar professions, hobbies, and so on. But when the parent is well known—even in a small, local way—this can be more devastating than sibling rivalry. Who hasn't heard of the preacher's kid—the wildest youngster on the block? Caroline Wyeth, the least known of the famous painting family, emerged in an interview last year because, she said, she was interested in "exploding the myth that we're just a big bunch of sweetie pies down here" (in the Pennsylvania village where the Wyeths live). Shirley MacLaine told a *Time* reporter that she and her brother, Warren Beatty, were so cowed by their extremely entertaining parents that "we'd just sit there and watch. It made both of us rather shy and one of our quests in life has been to overcome that shyness with self-expression."

What can parents do to reassure a child who feels he is hopelessly overshadowed by their arresting personalities or celebrity? Or better yet, to motivate him rather than paralyze him, or drive him to rebellion or escape?

A noted scientist, whose father was also well known, remembered that "the only way I could be with him at all was to accompany him to work." He felt that his mother had handled this very well: She had showed respect and love for her husband, but never made much of his accomplishment. "She was a teacher and highly sensitive to our needs. She felt this was important so we wouldn't feel overwhelmed."

It can help when parents play down parental achievements and emphasize the youngster's—but not so obviously that it's forced. It's not hard to make a child feel that his daddy or mommy is great, but that he or she too will be great in his or her own way. Dad's picture may be in the paper, but Junior's poem is taped to the kitchen wall and sent to relatives. Successful parents are always aware of the subtleties of a child's own temperament. They realize that setting a high standard of success can be as devastating for some as it is inspiring for others. One achiever put it this way: "My parents always just assumed I'd be a professional, like my father. And I interpreted that to mean I'd have to be a *superior* professional." For him, it worked.

Open communication

Communication is probably the most overworked word in the social sciences today. It's well known how hard it is to bare your feelings to those who can hurt you. Endless workshops in assertiveness training, handling relationships, sensitivity attest to this. Things were no different with the survey families. More than one mother remembered this as a major problem in the family. One said "keeping the lines of communication open" was her toughest challenge in raising an achieving daughter. Painter John Clem Clarke's mother told of acting as a channel between father and son for several years while the boy pursued a career in art against his father's strenuous objections. "John was finishing his first year of college when he expressed a desire to go into the art field, much to our surprise. His father was very disappointed and opposed it, as he had wished for a career in sports or anything *except* art. John played football in the Rose Bowl, then changed college to specialize in art. Then after graduating he spent three years studying art in Europe. All this time I was 'go-between' between John and his dad.... This is a very difficult situation to find oneself involved in... but we made it work." Although both parents did not support the child's interests, the mother's commitment to both family members was sufficient to cover the distance.

Why did she persist? Because of "John's ability to understand his needs and persuade me that he knew what he could do if we would just give him a chance." Needless to say, her son is now an acclaimed artist.

- *Communication and sharing in decision making* Not only is the act of communicating important, but the manner in which it's done enhances its flow. Researcher Glen Elder produced a paper with the weighty title of "Parental Power Legitimation and its Effect on the Adolescent," in which he reported on the types of power parents use on their children and connected it to how they communicated. He divided parents into three groups:

High power or "autocratic" parents did not allow their children to have their own opinions or to regulate their own behavior. Moderate power or "democratic" parents encouraged their children to participate in decisions relating to their behavior, but kept the final say themselves. Low power or "permissive" parents gave their children more influence in decisions about their behavior than the parents had.

Elder tested this idea, asking a large group of seventh-to-twelfth graders if their parents explained their decisions or rules to them, and how those decisions were made. This is what he found:

Democratic and permissive parents were more likely to explain rules to their children. ("The reason we want you to do this is...") than autocratic parents ("Just do as I say and don't ask questions"). The children who desired most often to be like their parents were raised by democratic explainers, the group with, presumably, the greatest parent-child involvement in decision-making. This would support the notion that the greater the interaction, the more likely the child will want to be like his parents. College orientation was also greatest in this group.

Permissive explainers on the other hand produced children who were most autonomous, with the strongest feelings of competence and self-reliance. At the other end of the scale, autocratic parents produced children who were most accepting of power, most passive, most indifferent to scholastic achievement.

Frequency of explanation was the critical factor. Children who seldom received parental explanation, regardless of the parental power level, were least likely to be autonomous. In fact, the less power the parents used, the more their explanations seemed to "foster a sense of self-confidence and independence in their children."

Once again, the survey mothers came in right on cue with the experts. "We never had a generation gap—my parents saw through my eyes as I saw through my children's eyes," said one mother, giving credit to where she learned mothering. Congresswoman Pat Schroeder's mother talked of "the importance of understanding through talk and discussion." Mrs. Gibson remembered, "People always said we were like brothers and sisters. There was no 'boss' in the house. Others commented on it to us."

Researchers studying single-parent families repeated the Elder experience. They found that in those families where the single parent communicates closely with the older children, involving them in family matters and decision making, the children often become more responsible and mature than those of comparable age in two-parent homes where they are shut out of the decision-making process and remain in a kind of "placeless" limbo between maturity and childhood.

- *Can you improve communication?* This is always hard at first, especially in families that are not talkative, or where the talk covers up real feelings. The major hurdle in creating open communication is not just to talk about things loaded with meaning and emotion, but to create an atmosphere in which such talk can happen safely.

  Once again, as parents, we set the example. If we can come to terms with an issue in open discussion, we can help our families do the same. Learning to discuss and admit deeply held anger, anxieties, conflicts, and resentments with your youngsters is valuable for the whole family. Probably the most important thing to remember is that nobody's perfect—and you don't have to be, either. This leaves the door always open for authentic and honest communication.

  Sociologist Robert Coles, author of a famous series on American children which includes the best-selling *Children of Crisis*, gave an example of this. The young son of a wealthy grower complained in school about the bad conditions of migrant pickers. His teachers sent him to a psychologist, who diagnosed various syndromes. Then his parents took another look at their youngster and realized they'd produced, as the father put it, "an actual believing Christian." Before long father was spearheading a move to improve the workers' lot, and mother had come out of the woodwork too. She stopped catering to her powerful husband and started voicing her own views on exploited labor and other matters. Thus one family changed its whole social stance thanks to open communication—but it didn't happen overnight.

- *Techniques* It's usually easier to try a new technique when a situation comes up that demands it. But if you want to use open communication in a crisis, don't wait for one. You can warm up merely by asking your children some questions they thought you'd never ask: Would you go to school if you didn't have to? give money to a beggar? ask your parents to stop smoking? stay at (or leave) a party where marijuana was being used? stand up for an unpopular kid if you thought he was right? go to war for your country?

    These questions were devised as techniques for value clarification by psychologist Sidney Simon. Asking them not only helps your children formulate their own opinions, it lets them know that you, too, are aware of matters that are tough to talk about, and are willing to hear their views. Teaching your children to declare themselves honestly by admitting your own weaknesses, and presenting an attitude of caring and listening—in which there are no "wrong" answers—can build a formidable groundwork to lean on when real storms hit the household.

Moral principles and religious precepts: learning to be a "good person"

This was one of the surprising findings of the survey. We had not expected the mothers to be so emphatic about the importance of ethical standards, but they were. We asked the mothers, "When your child was growing up, how important did you think it was for your child to (a) be a good person, (b) be independent, (c) be happy, (d) attain a standard of excellence or high achievement, and (e) be well liked?" They were given choices of very, somewhat, not very, and not at all. They were then asked, "Which did you consider *most* important?"

Over 80 percent of the mothers ranked "be a good person" as very important, and it far outranked the other options as the most important choice of all. Some felt teaching moral values was the chief contribution they'd made to their youngster's success. Scientist Floyd Bloom's mother put it in terms of "making him see right from wrong." Banker Clarence Barksdale's mother said, "We tried to have high ideals constantly before our children," and international urban planner Marietta Tree remembered "stressing the importance of contributing to the community," something she herself has done to an extraordinary degree. (Her daughter, Frances FitzGerald, has followed suit, writing first a Pulitzer Prize-winning study of Vietnam and then a ground-breaking critique of American history textbooks.)

Religion and religious training were also important to the survey mothers. Only a handful said they were "not at all religious." Nearly a third said they were very religious, all the rest described themselves as somewhat religious. Many spoke of it with deep conviction. Faye Dunaway's mother gave credit to her belief in God; Andrew Young's felt his religious training had been the major influence in his life; Judith Jamison's said "seeing to her religious training" was a contribution. Nearly half the youngsters went to Sunday school or had other religious instruction. Michael Crichton's mother remembered these lessons as a valuable catalyst for her son, raising questions that led to long debates at home after church which she felt were important in increasing Michael's awareness of others at an early age.

This seems to be the main moral message: Be aware of others. Our mothers wanted their children to be successes, for sure, but not at the expense of stepping on others. The message crossed all faiths, even generations as shown by these remarks from two mothers and an achiever, one each from a Protestant, Catholic, and Jewish family:

I don't care what religion you have, but believe something! Religion teaches you to be more understanding, and have empathy for other people. It makes a big difference.

The current tendency is to be permissive. I have caught myself along the way, realizing that with my children at the age they are now, about half the time they are going to be with me is over. I want to expose them to my values. I feel myself not wanting to lose the opportunity to tell them what's right or wrong in a given situation and these things come out in conversations all the time. Once one of them gave a party, and didn't want to invite a particular child. I heard them discussing this. It took me about a day to "come to," and I knew I had to insist she include him, so she did. The child's mother called and thanked us. It was the first party in a whole series her youngster had been invited to. I know my daughter realized she had done the right thing and she was happy. That is exactly what my mother would do—she'd find the one kid in the class who was unpopular and she'd say, "You call him up and invite him over." And of course we would.

My father always would bring in elderly and poor people on Christmas and he would take care of them first. Shoes, comfortable shoes, for the old people would be the first thing; nowadays one might see forty gifts under a tree but not then. We never cared about material things, we just shared everything. Our family life was the same thing; the boys' father would always spend his time with them, take them fishing or on a picnic. I was always there too. In our family it was always the feeling for others that was the important aspect in our religion, and today my sons have that—for each other and for everyone else too.

A second look at these remarks shows us more than just that moral precepts are important to achieving families: "She had done the right thing and she was happy" (parental reinforcement for ethical behavior); "These things come out in conversations all the time" (open communication); "He would always spend his time with them....I was there too" (sharing time as a family). All these show how good family atmospheres are created and spontaneously express themselves.

- *Permissiveness versus values* One of the trickier problems of childrearing is to avoid confusing permissiveness with abdication. There's a big difference. We've described how democratic and permissive parents, those who explain things and leave some decisions up to their children, tend to raise more achievers than do autocratic parents—but they don't leave *everything* up to their children.

    Many parents, however, do fall into the pattern of just "letting things happen" where moral issues are concerned, simply because they can be so complex. Parents often find themselves unable to discuss such critical should I/shouldn't I issues as drugs, alcohol, sex or even cheating and fair play, especially with older children. This can make the parents uneasy and fill the children with anxiety and indecision, often leaving them no option but to follow the crowd, which probably consists of children of other abdicating parents.

    The solution to this dilemma is to develop a clear parental or family value system together that can help sort things out and provide answers where none may be apparent. Most parents follow an informal, unstated value system all the time in dealing with such simple things as returning items to local stores, tipping in restaurants, doing their fair share of caring for sick relatives or handling neighborhood duties. Children see this sort of behavior in action and can follow the examples. But when mother comes to grips with something like, "Can I have a career and still care properly for my children?" she's wrestling with a should I/shouldn't I quandary every bit as difficult for her as theirs are for them. Besides, her priority decision will affect the whole family. Yet, how many children see her going through the decision-making process?

When you work through these questions together, reviewing your priorities and the values they reflect, explaining to your growing children why you do the things you do, you're giving the youngsters a foundation on which they can begin to clarify their values and priorities too. Opening up such a channel of communication also makes it easier for them to come to you with their serious questions. They'll know you won't evade the issue, or deliver an ultimatum, but will instead help them think it through.

Finally, you can show in your behavior that you have the strength of character to resist the crowd. You can't tell your children they can't have any drinks or drugs, and then come reeling home from a party yourself the next night, and expect the message to stick. Your example when it comes to upholding ethical values cannot be overestimated. Where children are concerned, their basic feeling of justice is challenged. Since the negative messages get passed down right along with the positive ones, it seems better to admit your slips while holding out the ideal of perfection, explaining that you're still striving to meet it, too!

The problem-solving alliance

Inevitably, families must deal with major stresses and problems from outside. The family faced with a continuing stress, like poverty, or an acute situation such as a parent's illness, can react either by turning on itself or by banding together. Let's consider both responses in hypothetical situations: Mr. Green has been laid off from his job of fifteen years as an airplane designer. His wife, watching him become depressed, feels edgy, and nags him about finding another job and helping her decorate the house, a project they've been working on for years but which she now feels impatient to complete. As the couple spends more time together, their squabbles multiply. When the children enter the room, they are apt to get scolded for little things or sent off so "we can finish what we're talking about." Mr. Green begins to frequent a bar just to get away from the hassle at home; and the children, feeling tense, become less cheerful and increasingly whiny. Gradually the family begins to splinter, to drift apart, each member feeling more and more lonely in the family setting.

The White family, faced with the same problem, deals with the blow very differently. Mrs. White, a giving person, responds to her husband's distress by suggesting they take a trip to his favorite fishing place for a long weekend, knowing it is something he loves, and that it will give him an opportunity to relax and think, gaining perspectives that often seemed unreachable during his hectic work life. Their four children accompany them, joining in a fine experience, but also each having time to be alone and reflect in the peace of the wilderness. In the days following their trip, Mrs. White encourages her husband to think over a number of different job possibilities and to take time to talk them over with helpful friends and contacts, as well as with her. They talk about this a great deal, and often the children enter the discussion, both when guests are present—and they have many—or at mealtimes when the whole family is together. During what becomes a lengthy period of unemployment, the family makes arrangements to see themselves through the crisis. Extras like decorating the house and eating out are postponed, and each member of the family thinks of things he or she could do without. A teenage son takes a job at the supermarket after school; a daughter doubles her babysitting. Mrs. White, who had planned to return to school for a degree, instead takes a job to cover expenses while her husband looks for the right opportunity.

She makes a point of finding work that gives her useful experiences for her future studies along with that important paycheck.

Coping with any major change, above the daily pushes and pulls of life, is a tall order for a system composed of mere human beings. The Greens fell apart. The Whites were saved by their spontaneous formation of a problem-solving alliance when the bomb dropped. They worked together, kept each others' spirits up, and didn't make Dad feel like a failure. The feeling was entirely one of a temporary rather than permanent setback. No one gave up a dream; instead they kept their dreams warm by adjusting plans for the future.

This problem-solving alliance can come into play on problems arising from within the family, such as sibling rivalries or a child's school crises, or from without, as the father's loss of work we've just described.

The survey families certainly had their share of problems. One out of five families had a member who was seriously ill; some had lost a son, daughter, or father. A few had had to endure the difficulties of a grandparent, father, or sibling with a long-term illness. Many others suffered economic adversity growing out of the Depression. Twenty-five percent had decreasing incomes during their child-rearing years, certainly a major stress.

Mrs. Gibson remembers when her husband's salary was cut, forcing them to leave "a brand-new home and furniture," her first home of her own. Looking back, she says, "It was a blow. I cried for a year." Do her children remember? She thinks Kenneth does, because "he never forgot a thing." During the time the family lived in one room, she believes they learned some valuable lessons about getting along with others— "you just had to"—and developed a strong sense of family solidarity.

The Gibsons developed a powerful alliance, further expressed by Mrs. Gibson's response to how they handled the children's desire, typical of every economic level, to have whatever all the other kids had. "We always told them, 'If you ever want anything, come to us. If we don't have it, we'll explain why, or we'll try to get it.... Even if you have nothing else to give, you can give them that.'" Later she said, "Whatever they wanted, we usually saw that they got it. Kenneth says he never knew we were poor."

Painter Larry Bell's mother recalled that her husband—a "wonderful and supportive man in every way"—had suffered a severe heart attack when her boys were still young. She had to step into the breach at her husband's infant business, and remembers her children's behavior gratefully: "They were loving, good children and I was fortunate....They helped *me*. I couldn't have survived without their love and encouragement....We were lucky we had each other."

Can problems be a plus for achievers? The uses of adversity

In handling problems such as these, and those of loneliness or "being different" or "not having a father like the other kids had," the children of our sample and their families seemed to pull together. These mothers and fathers, or mothers alone, were able to reinforce their children's capacity and determination to succeed in the teeth of adversity.

Is there a connection? We've already discussed superkids, and Freud's notion of compensation could also support the idea that children experiencing early hardships can resolve to overcome, or compensate for, them in adulthood. The many rags-to-riches legends in our culture are evidence of those who did succeed against adversity of all kinds—poverty, disability, abuse, or illiteracy as well as loss or serious illness of a parent or sibling.

Though one could hardly recommend misfortune as the road to achievement—especially in our sample, where so much that was positive was going on—the achievers did show a forceful response to adversity. Marjorie Guthrie regretted that the long illness of her husband, famed poet-balladeer Woody Guthrie, had kept her occupied and both parents away from their four children for long periods at a time. Yet their father's legacy is clear in what they grew up to be: dancer, music teacher, musician, and songwriter.

When asked the source of her son's motivation, John Updike's mother said, "I think our family's predicament was motivating; a three-generation family, and all had fallen down. There was a need for us to be picked up. He saw that...."

Ultimately, how a family handles problems is probably the best reflection of the family's atmosphere. One achiever had this truly impressive memory of how things were at her house:

Our family had this attitude toward problems, this forward motion. For example, when my sisters were very ill, or when father got cancer. Never, "Why us?" No sense of despair, but always, "It will work out." This same attitude had to do with problems in school and so forth. Everything was seen as a challenge. The message was, "You've got what it takes." No one ever spread worries around.

To behave in a way that leaves your children a memory—and a model—like that twenty years hence is really worth trying for; it is genuine achievement as a parent.

7. Raising children for self-reliance: a key to achievement

Up to now in this book we've been describing what could be called a parenting "style." This comprised strong early nurturing, including parental involvement, support, enthusiasm, and commitment. It seems paradoxical to suggest that if a child who has been devotedly nurtured in infancy and early childhood is taught self-reliance at a rather young age, the result is greater maturity and self-motivation. Nevertheless, a great deal of evidence supports this view, including our survey results.

Whether it was described as self-discipline, self-reliance, taking responsibility, being independent, showing initiative, determination, or even maturing early, this was the one factor that all agreed on: Almost without exception, parents, experts, and especially achievers gave it the chief credit for success. As some of them said:

"Perhaps the earliest memories I have are of being a stubborn, determined child....No one could have deflected me from my path."

"I stick with a project until it's done. Wrote ten drafts of my book in one year—no one believes me. I love to work and I'm always doing something."

"My parents were very disciplined....I always had lots of energy, and was rambunctious....I've never known it any other way. When I was fourteen, I was practicing six hours a day....I may be more determined and focused than others who have been less successful. I was raised in the midst of a family attitude of success."

"Inner discipline was very important. A child has to cultivate his own, not have it forced on him. And work was very important in our home."

Crossing the bridge to self-discipline

We spoke of the bridge of motivation that talented children must cross to achieve mastery of their creative gifts and take them into adult life. Parents can encourage; admire; provide lessons, materials, and classses; but there comes a time when the child must pursue the artistic or scientific gift on his own. This is really a bridge from parental discipline and influence to self-discipline, where the child learns to listen to his own inner voice for motivation.

That discussion was in the context of talented children, but here we see it as occurring in the backgrounds of— and becoming a habit of—every kind of achiever: senators, bankers, entertainers, educators, theologians, musicians, writers, scientists. They seem to have been able to actualize their need to achieve as adults through the inner discipline they learned in childhood. The transition may be characteristic of adolescence but, as with the bridge for talented children, the underpinnings are laid much earlier.

Teaching patterns of self-reliance

The sum and substance of most achievement is the willingness to make sacrifices in order to attain a goal: long hours of practice, extra projects, difficult subjects, overtime work—often at the expense of what other people think would be more fun. The fixing on a goal, which spurs us to make the sacrifices, can happen early or late in life, and be inspired by any source: a parent, a teacher, a neighbor, a book one read, a movie one saw. This inspiration plays such a special and important part that we devote the next chapter to discussing the impact of role models, mentors, and "the dream" in motivating achievers.

But no matter what the goal, without the habits and style of self-discipline, the simple know-how of making sacrifices with positive instead of negative feelings, it may never come to pass.

Self-discipline for achievement is really a set of values relating to individual behavior. Although connected to the system of moral principles that covered being a good person, which also involves duty and sacrifice, this set of values is more closely linked to work habits, organization of time, careful accomodation of all elements in one's life (family, play, work, solitude), and that very important sense of completion: getting things done!

Can self-discipline be taught? Perhaps not like the alphabet or fractions, but probably much more than you realize. Even though this seems to be an inner gift, there are actually many things parents can do in everyday life to enhance its development. According to our data, these seemed to be the basic components:

1. *Setting an example.* Many achievers spoke of imitating self-reliant parents; but even if you think you're not self-disciplined there are things you can do that will leave a positive impression.

2. *Continued love and support.* This was virtually universal among the survey mothers—not just a blind

acceptance of anything or everything a child wants to do, but showing you're on the child's side in spite of problems or infractions. This gives the child security to make the experiments involved in learning autonomy without anxiety.

3. *Granting autonomy.* We've described how important this can be in infancy. Ongoing willingness, especially in the adolescent period, to let children discover things and make judgments on their own later.

4. *Instilling a sense of the child's capabilities.* This was expressed in many forms of parental behavior: how early they expected their children to look after themselves; what they expected them to do around the house; how they expected them to handle money. How they expected them to perform at school, a big part of this, is handled in Chapter 9.

5. *Accentuating the positive and disciplining to maintain self-esteem.* Rewarding good behavior and emphasizing positive accomplishments more often than punishing negative ones seemed to be the survey mothers' secret to successful discipline. They also chose punishments designed to encourage self-reliance rather than fear.

All these were used by the survey parents in helping their children gain the self-reliance needed to maintain the achievement motive through the bumpy years of adolescence and on into an achieving adulthood.

Setting an example

Rosalyn Yalow remembers her father: "He was always home for dinner at 6 o'clock sharp, and there was a saying at our house that if you didn't read the paper by 7 o'clock it would be thrown out." She cites his efficiency as being responsible for the way she is: "I always operated that way. When the children were little, I would drive them to Florida for vacation and all the way it would be up at 6, bags packed and so forth. So the children are just naturally organized too. I never really taught them."

Congresswoman Pat Schroeder's mother remembered teaching her youngster "to finish projects started, to plan and organize....She was very quick with many ideas. I helped her to sort and plan and decide which were the most beneficial."

There is no doubt that what we do as parents carries great weight in how our children will act when they grow up. Here we've seen two examples from the achievers, and all of us can remember similar impressions of our own organized or unorganized parents.

You may not see yourself as disciplined, but things are probably going on in your household that will promote self-reliance in your youngster. There's the awesome power of cultural values and customs. No one knows this better than those who have grown up outside them. In his moving book, *Beyond Black and White*, psychiatrist James Comer discussed the dilemma of minority children who reach maturity without any examples of goal-oriented behavior to prepare them to achieve, as contrasted with those who do:

Long before entering school, many youngsters from stable families (which may contain either one parent or two) have been developing styles and skills necessary to acquiring a sense of industry and the desire to work. Simply being in a household where people are regularly getting up, organizing to be on time and preparing for work transmits the notion that work and constancy are important and rewarding. Many youngsters at their play type or teach like mommy or carry a stethoscope or a wrench like daddy, practicing to become workers. Various aspects of middle-income living, such as goal setting, time orientation, and expectation of stability, give a direction and discipline to living that develop goal-directed and problem-solving behavior.

The capacity for sustained work in our society is, for better or worse, also developed through mastering the basic academic skills and maneuvering through the social system of a public school. The child who can maneuver with relative success wins praise, develops a sense of adequacy and a need to be involved in productive activities. Failure in school may do just the opposite.

We are certainly not suggesting that you make no effort beyond going through your daily routine to encourage self-reliance in your youngster. All the other ways of behaving we'll describe, which don't require being organized but which do demand awareness, can be useful. But your example remains central to the objective.

Love and autonomy: self-reliance in a supportive environment

If we go back to Erik Erikson's early stages, we'll remember they are (1) trust, (2) autonomy, "the beginning exercise of choice," and (3) initiative, where the child wants to be aggressive without feeling guilt and jealousy toward others. Once the child has established basic trust, he can move on to autonomy and exercising his own initiative. If he's been lucky enough to have a mother who granted him autonomy and encouraged his initiative, he may remember it gratefully.

Many achievers stressed the importance of this love/autonomy combination, saying their family's greatest contribution to their success may have been in "letting me go," "leaving me alone," or "letting me follow my own instincts." As the children got older, and began to hear their own inner voices, they started wanting to do things that weren't what everyone else on the block was doing. We have overwhelming evidence that parental support at such junctures can make a crucial difference to the child's feelings, reinforcing his self-reliance and self-confidence, and making him better able to do the job required to reach his goal. This is true no matter when these milestones come along in life. Daniel Callahan, who left a successful academic career in midlife to found The Hastings Center shared this wonderful memory with us:

My parents were very different; my father [a newspaperman] was gregarious, an entrepreneur always giving money to start or stop something. He moved around a lot, often to my mother's distress. She was more inclined to be anxious. They were permissive, not in the sense of ignoring kids, but rather that we should be able to get out and explore, travel....There was never any pressure to be any particular thing. They were not intellectuals; when I told them I wanted to get a PhD in philosophy, it was inexplicable to them, but they supported me, all through my education, not the way some parents say today, "OK, we'll support you until you are 18, or through college." They just gave me their support. And when I started the Hastings Center at the age of 39, with six kids, my academic friends didn't back me at all—they couldn't see how I could do it; my father, on the other hand, was thrilled—the entrepreneur again. He felt it was great that his son was starting something new. I asked if he felt any qualms about the risks himself. "The thing couldn't help but succeed, unless we really fouled it up," was his attitude. I never felt any insecurity or anxiety, even as a child. My mother may have, with my father's investments, but I got the message: "Whatever you do, you'll do well," and the permissiveness to go out and do it.

Instilling a sense of the child's capabilities

The first clue to this is that the survey mothers gave responsibility to their children early. As we know, they expected them to do things for themselves, such as know their way around the neighborhood, put away their things, do homework, and so on when the children were still quite young. Different from granting the child freedom to make decisions on his own, this was a series of demands that the child be responsible for performance of adult-like tasks.

Responsibility implies independence. Three-fourths of the mothers considered it "very important" for a child to be independent, while only about half felt it important for a child to be well liked. The mother of a political figure said that if she could rear her son again, she would "teach him to be more assertive, not to try to please other people, but himself"—in a word, to be independent.

This emphasis on responsibility, on independence, on autonomy, is interesting in view of studies comparing the parents of low-achieving children with those of high achievers. The parents of low achievers typically emphasize conformity and obedience. They see themselves essentially as dictators, ever alert to keep their naturally unruly public in tow. The parents of high-achieving youngsters, on the other hand, are much less concerned about enforcing rules. To them, being a parent means helping the child grow into a self-reliant, responsible adult.

- *Contributing to the household* This emphasis on handling responsibility is well displayed by the fact that high-achieving children are expected not just to contribute to the household, but to contribute at an early age, and with a specific point of view. More than a matter of just doing chores, it entailed an unspoken sense of participation and obligation. It was a factor in all families in the survey.

Children are challenged by assuming roles where they can see they are making a contribution, whether it be farm chores or child care and homemaking tasks. The parent, of course, cannot abandon responsibility to the child; it must be given in a protective environment. A recent study showed that in homes where mothers left responsibility for younger children completely in the hands of older ones, the burden was so crippling it often left the older youngsters unable to function as adults. Forced to assume authority before they ever experienced life without it, they could not adapt to a world where they were not in charge. Such children also usually performed their responsibilities in angry fear of parental reprisal. The combination could be disastrous for their own children: Deprived of nurturing at an early age, they never learned how to nurture others. This experience was noted in underprivileged families where, sometimes for generations, the big kids have had to look after the little ones and nobody's had a real childhood.

The survey respondents seem to have had a unifying point of view about this despite their educational, social, or financial background. Robert Coles has written that upper-class children are "taught reasons to feel proud of themselves, to feel grateful for what their parents have done... against great odds and with considerable self-sacrifice." Along with this attitude goes a sense of obligation to the community, prompted by an awareness of the political, economic, and social power that accompanies affluence. As one of our survey mothers put it, "Much is expected of those to whom much is given."

In fact, some of our subjects were somewhat apologetic for having been born well-off. They were anxious to stress to their children the importance of "working for a living," "picking up after oneself—even when there were servants to do it"—and not seeing oneself as too special "in spite of horses and trips to Europe."

In contrast, the poorest families were quite comfortable about sharing their economic histories, but without any corresponding guilt. They too were proud of themselves and grateful for the way they had managed to stay together and afloat against great odds and with sacrifices; emphasizing how they had helped each other, and the virtues of discipline and hard work. In an affluent family the message might be, "Pick up your room because it's your responsibility to be neat and not make extra work for others." In poorer homes the message was, "It's your responsibility because it's got to be done and there's no one else to do it." In both cases, the idea was that everyone contributes.

Although most of our respondents were neither rich nor poor, these examples from the extremes are significant because they show that similar values were held right across the sample.

- *Jobs and handling money* We know that survey children, as do most others as they get a bit older, babysat, worked in stores, had paper routes, or even wrote articles (Michael Crichton) or played music (Sarah Fryer Leibowitz, Burt Bacharach) to earn money. To find out how early survey parents had introduced their youngsters to financial responsibility, we asked them if they had given their children weekly allowances; if so, at what ages and for what purpose: (1) to pay their own expenses (lunches, carfare), (2) to spend on luxuries, recreation, or (3) to save in the bank or at home.

Over 60 percent of the mothers remembered giving allowances. Many couldn't remember when they had begun this practice, but a couple started training their children with money as early as four or five, for luxuries and savings. About half the rest began allowances at early grade-school levels (six to eight) and most of the rest around early adolescence (twelve to fourteen).

Purposes were about evenly divided, with a slightly larger number stipulating the lunch/carfare choice. Many mothers checked all three choices, and several indicated "no restrictions." We can conclude that since the majority were expected to handle money by their teens, and many a good deal earlier, this introduction to one of life's realities could also have encouraged that most basic kind of self-reliance: financial.

Accentuating the positive: praise over blame

"My mother is an extremely supportive person; we always used to say we would get complimented for coming down to breakfast in the morning," says Joe Lieberman. "Why does this motivate?" he wonders. "Why doesn't it have the opposite effect? It certainly motivated me."

How did our mothers encourage initiative and responsibility? We asked, "When your child was young (under 12) and fulfilled your expectations or was 'good,' how did you react?" The mothers relied heavily on praise and, at least when the children were young, on hugs and kisses. Three-fourths of the mothers said that they praised their children, and 61 percent showed their approval with physical affection. Only 12 percent of the mothers admitted they sometimes "did nothing at all..." lest they make an act seem special.

It's easy, of course, to take a child's efforts for granted. But numerous studies have demonstrated that this can lead to trouble. Take the case of teachers who ignore students when they are in their seats, working hard, and pay attention to them only when they are fiddling at their desks. Result: The students spend more and more time fiddling. When these teachers are made aware of their own behavior and begin rewarding the children for behaving well, the students show remarkable improvement.

The parents of our achievers seemed to know that if you ignore a child's efforts often enough, he's likely to quit trying. Still, many parents fall into the "negative habit" of paying no attention when children play quietly, do their homework or perform some chore without being reminded. Instead, they take notice only when the child is disruptive.

Some parents also fall into the trap of pointing out a child's inadequacies rather than focusing on and being pleased about his progress. When, for example, a child ties his shoelace for the first time and the parent reties it to show how it could have been done better, the youngster will probably be discouraged. The message is, "You failed." Only six parents questioned said they sometimes responded to a child's efforts by showing "how it could have been done better."

The emphasis, then, was on the positive, on rewarding desirable, responsible behavior, rather than punishing misconduct and failure. But since all children go astray sometimes, what did our interviewees do then? "When your child was young (under 12)," we asked, "and misbehaved or disappointed you, how did you react?" About three-fourths of the mothers showed their disappointment and pointed out what they expected of the child. Half "scolded or spanked," but several of these respondents crossed out "spanked" or wrote in the margin that they rarely if ever spanked their children. Only two answered that they wouldn't show any feelings about the incident.

The mothers were capable, then, of being punitive. But the emphasis both in rewarding and in punishing the child seemed to be on giving feedback about his or her progress on the road toward productive adulthood. Praise and kisses were ways of saying, "I'm so proud of you when you behave this way, you're doing so well!"

Expressing disappointment or even spanking a child were ways of saying, "I'm ashamed of you. You are capable of much more than this."

Why is the positive rather than negative approach so effective? Most experts who work with parents and children feel it develops self-esteem in a growing child, and that this is essential for later confidence and motivation.

- *Discipline and self-esteem* Carol Tucker Foreman's mother would agree. She linked motivation to discipline when she said her most important contribution to her achievers' success had been "keeping them motivated and moving in the right direction. They have all had plenty of discipline and love. When discipline is seasoned with love, a child's sense of personal worth is not diminished and his ego is not shattered."

    When asked to rate their approach to discipline on a scale from very strict to very lenient, the survey mothers avoided the extremes, choosing "strict" and "lenient" in about equal numbers. Since closeness and self-reliance were key components in family life, this only reinforces the point that the goal for the child was not humiliation nor penance, but rather the attainment of his or her own self-control.

We already know that though mothers did most of the disciplining (as 84 percent said), father was in agreement. That some mothers deplored the "wait till your father comes home" technique of discipline only further emphasizes their point of view.

In his book, *Priceless Gifts*, Daniel Sugarman discusses self-esteem as one of the critically important "gifts" a child receives as he grows up. Explaining how our feelings about ourselves tend to reflect appraisals of others who were close to us, Dr. Sugarman makes an important point about the maturing child:

> We can't embarrass a child and then expect him or her to grow up with a healthy sense of self-esteem.
>
> Many tribes of American Indians, for example, felt that it was extremely important for their children to grow up with a solid sense of self-esteem.
>
> According to one story, an Indian chief and a missionary sat down for a long talk in order to reconcile their differences. They spoke about many things, and at one point the Indian asked the missionary, "Why don't white folks want their sons to grow up to be braves?"
>
> "Of course, we want our sons to be braves," the missionary replied. "It's very important to white people that our sons become braves!"
>
> "Then how come I once saw a white man slapping his son?" asked the chief. "Every Indian knows that if you don't treat your son with honor, he can never honor himself...."

Many of the survey mothers elaborated on how this process felt to them. In Kenneth Gibson's home, "We were very strict. We always *agreed*, although I was the chief disciplinarian. We used little punishment, mostly disapproval. I don't think a child over three or four should ever be touched. Take away some privileges and *get it over with quick!"*

The road to adolescence: parents and children in transit

Adolescence is the period when children learn to become adults, to act on their own, to become (one hopes) responsible citizens. It's clear that most survey parents tried to establish their youngsters in self-reliant patterns before they reached adolescence; but quite naturally, arrival at this gateway created some reversals, as it does in most families. We've already mentioned the parents who gave their children years of lessons only to find the interest abandoned overnight in favor of some new passion. Children who had been well behaved can become a little wild; rambunctious chatterboxes can become introspective.

Sometimes it's mother who switches gears. Researcher Sheila Feld discovered this when she went back to a group of teenage boys who had been tested for achievement when they were small. Their mothers had also been rated for behavior, such as the granting of autonomy and so on. Feld found that the boys' need to achieve remained basically stable right through from childhood to adolescence, but their mothers' attitudes toward independent accomplishment seemed to reverse! Of course now the mothers were being questioned on issues such as dating, showing leadership, staying home alone overnight—quite different from picking up your own room or going to the store alone. Perhaps the mothers were just reacting to their sons' behavior: The mother who didn't stress independence when her boy was ten may have felt forced to when her son, merely responding to her early training, was still a dependent mama's boy at sixteen with no desire to get ahead in the world. Similarly, the mother who had stressed independence for her little boy may have been faced with a teenage Romeo, man of the world, who needed to be reined in occasionally.

- *Storms: the typical weather* The situation described by Feld is representative of many encountered by parents and children in establishing the degree of independence to be accorded the growing teenager. Both sides are continuously gaining or giving ground in a constant process of adaptation. The child's need to assert himself and the parents' recognition of the need to set limits make this not only appropriate, but even valuable. Forty years ago Harvard University undertook a study of its alumni to learn more about adjustment over the life cycle. Now known as the Grant Study, this innovative research reached the conclusion that a smooth adolescence is not necessarily normal, nor predictive of a successful life as an adult. Anna Freud, daughter of the famed analyst and a world-renowned child specialist in her own right, believed this to be true as well; and recent research at the University of California tends to confirm that a stormy adolescent period is associated with better adaptation and controls in later life.

  The very rare teenager who is well balanced and controlled may just be shutting off adolescent emotional processes which can resurface and lead to problems in later years. This is the sort of thing that can make a run-of-the-mill midlife transition into a midlife crisis. So if you're resisting this churning emotional sea, or looking for an island of calm in its midst, give up. It's part of the process for both you and your child, whether or not he or she is, or is going to be, an achiever.

- *Maintaining achievement effort through adolescence* Many parent-child relationships do go on the rocks in adolescence, at least for a time. Whatever the mood of the moment—positive or negative—there's often a connection between the child's achievement and parental behavior.

  The main arena where teenagers find direction is

that of personal achievement. In these years, one suddenly has the emotional and physical independence to be able to demonstrate impressive accomplishments—in clubs, student government, sports, the arts, or the classroom. Spurts of achievement are often rewarded so immediately and meaningfully that the child is propelled into greater accomplishment. A boy takes up the trumpet and becomes a musical celebrity in school. A girl acts in the school play and her self-image is a little different ever after. An essay published in the school paper, top honors in a contest—these are not just prizes, they become important motivators.

The way parents, teachers, and other adults and peers react to these early flashes of talent is all-important. An art student having a hard time getting encouragement for his work in an all-business family may either feel reluctance to continue or resent the extra effort he must make to overcome the resistance—both negative reactions. Compare this to the teenage comic who receives a tape recorder to immortalize his best routines: He knows his talents are appreciated and that his individuality and self-determination are respected—even admired. Such actions speak far louder than words, and as children get older they become even more sensitive to these gestures. Rosalyn Yalow's mother told of taking her daughter to the bank, at age twelve, to open an account. The bank refused, saying she was too young. "I told them she was in high school, and if she was able to manage that, she could certainly manage a bank account. They opened one."

In a story for *McCall's*, journalist Barbara G. Harrison showed that John Travolta's parents shared this attitude:

John dropped out of high school in the tenth grade, when he was sixteen—with his parents' approval. He promised Sam and Helen [his parents] that if he didn't make his mark in show business in a year, he'd be back home....He shared a cold-water flat in New York's Hell's Kitchen with his sister Ann. Within a year John was making commercials. When he was eighteen, he landed a part in the road company of Grease.... *And the rest, as they say, is history.*

Sam: *"We never said to Johnny, 'Why don't you become a priest like your cousin Frankie?' We never told him to be a doctor or a lawyer; we never wanted him to be anything but what he wanted to be. You know why so many stars don't seem to have any past or any parents? Because they never got permission to go out on their own. It takes a long time to make it in show business, and when a kid is out on the road making no money, his parents think he's a bum. We knew Johnny wasn't a bum. He knew he could always count on us. We looked after him even after he left home."*

These recollections bring out something you may have already observed: many of the reference points for training in self-reliance are virtually graduated versions of the components of gifted mothering. You can see several here: high expectations and belief in the child's future; encouraging talents; accentuating the positive; and finally, the crucial granting of autonomy in a loving and supportive environment.

8. Inspirations for achievement: role models, mentors, and the dream

Both of my parents were very encouraging by nature, and as an only child I reaped all the encouragement they had to give. The town and time also conduced to an innocent indulgence of a small person's dreams, and the supply of fuel, from Walt Disney movies to detective novels in the local city library, never ran short. Many teachers, beginning with the artist across the street, Mr. Clint Shilling, and continuing through a long line of English teachers of whom Mrs. Florence Schrack deserves especial mention, were mentors. My mother was mentor number one in the matter of art, my father in the matter of life and reality. At the age of thirteen I was moved to a farm where I had extra amounts of solitude to entertain. *Adversity, in the form of allergies and financial insecurity, visited me in stimulating but not overwhelming amounts. Adversity in immunological doses has its uses; more than that crushes. Religion was and is a helpful peripheral presence, giving me hopefulness and a sense of reward beyond the immediate and a suspicion of intrinsic excellence as an ultimate standard. I think a certain number of children now will motivate themselves, as long as the society can offer some reward for achievement.*

That was novelist John Updike's comprehensive and appealing answer to our request for who—or what—he remembered as motivating him to become the successful writer he is today. Most of us, after a moment's reminiscence, are surprised to realize how clearly we remember who or what inspired our youthful dreams, which may ultimately have brought us to where we are today. It's not always easy to pinpoint any one factor, as Updike's look backward shows, but among the many factors involved, there are almost sure to be a few adults who set us examples.

These examples—or role models, as they're called—set images for us of the basic pursuits of life: how we'll grow up to act and live, and what we'll grow up to do. They help form our behavior, beliefs, life-styles, and careers.

Parents as role models

Without doubt, parents are the outstanding role models we have in terms of how we'll act and live. Whether we recognize it or not, they are the living embodiment of values for us. Just as a son will pick up love of music or sports from sharing experiences with his father, so will he absorb his ways of dealing with people and work: impatience and disrespect or understanding and concern; workaholic isolation from the family or warm involvement with life; step-by-step progress toward a goal or wild risk taking.

The kind of homes we have, clothes we wear, friends we enjoy, politics we espouse, leisure activities we indulge in, books we read, colleges we attend, even pictures we hang are reflective of a desire to replicate or reject the homes we came from. Usually it's a blend of both.

Parents are often role models in terms of careers, too. Many children of teachers become teachers, children of lawyers and doctors become lawyers and doctors, and so on. We found this to be true of a number of the survey families. In many cases the climate of success around the household for such vocations encourages the child to follow them too. He or she has had a special kind of advance training in the field from babyhood, in addition to simply wanting to emulate the beloved and powerful parent.

This influence also crosses sex lines. The Barany boys' mother and father are both scientists, and there's John Updike's memory of being influenced by his mother, who is also a writer. We have many more examples of daughters following their fathers in careers, doubtless because until recently fathers tended to be the only ones who had them—as we think of them today, that is. A few generations back there was hardly a family without its maiden aunt schoolteacher, missionary, or dressmaker, but no one called them career women. There are obvious ones, such as Jane Fonda and Candice Bergen, but there are also Margot Hennig's less visible managerial women; nearly all were influenced and coached by their businessman fathers.

It was also true in single-parent homes. Whoever the "career" parent may be, or if one parent is playing both career and homemaking roles, the child will invariably pick up behaviors that he or she sees at home.

Other role models

Teachers, neighbors, and other relatives also served as role models. They gave children the opportunity to see how other adults conducted themselves in life-style and careers. A boy whose father is a plumber might never know what a pilot's life is like if not for the neighbor or uncle (or aunt!) who is one. There's the man up the street who runs the camera store, collects stamps, and has visited twenty countries; and the lady next door with six children who makes her own clothes and has a fabulous garden. Think of the impact of such people on a child who has never left his home state, or who has no brothers or sisters. Children from quiet families spend time with noisy ones; a bookish youngster finds a special friend in the librarian. Even if the role model is someone we've read about in a book or seen on stage or in a film, it's still a powerful depiction of the sort of grown-up we could choose to be.

Role models for success

Recent research shows that some celebrities can be powerful role models, too; not only because they symbolize the culture's desired goals of money and fame, but also because their stories of success over impossible odds make others willing to try.

Early identifications or associations with successful people can help children see that great achievers aren't demigods but real people. A survey mother illustrated this: "On a visit to a prominent relative when my son was about twelve, he commented, 'We shouldn't be here. These are important people. Let's go home.' I explained as well as I could that he could be important too, someday, if he chose to be." That explanation may have changed the boy's idea about himself and about what he could become.

Any of these nonparental role models represent an additional, potent resource, especially for those of us who do not grow up in the kind of super family where we can chat with composers and diplomats over Sunday dinner. A general responsiveness to inspiring figures, wherever they're found, can greatly increase the range of possibilities for potentially achieving children. Considering the development of the achievers in our sample, it appears that their early belief (which they got from their parents) that they could do or be anything, reinforced with positive adult models to choose from, helped give them both the matter and the manner for achieving in their own right.

Mentors and the dream

Role models are those people who make us say, "When I grow up, I wanna be..." Dr. Daniel Levinson of Yale, author of the widely-read study *The Seasons of a Man's Life*, describes two other factors besides role models that motivate people to succeed at careers. This is what "to succeed" still means to most of us, though our survey showed that if we learn to be successful *people* we have a much better chance of being successful in our work—or in anything else we might undertake.

Dr. Levinson's factors are *mentors* and *the dream*. *Mentors* are usually people already in the field. They are teachers, coaches, givers of information, advice, and direction. They show us how it's done. *The dream* is that living, powerful picture of our future selves that we have in our minds which starts—and keeps—us working toward that goal of success and full capability.

Dr. Levinson shows that it is hard to work toward anything without a dream. Many achievers remember their dreams of glory vividly. Singer Donna Summer said on television recently:

"I saw how my parents struggled and I said to myself, 'There has *got* to be a better way than this.' Then I heard Mahalia Jackson and I knew, '*That* is what I want....'" My mother would laugh, but my father took me aside and taught me....Then, later, I remember hearing my voice, not being sure it was even mine—and knowing that I was blessed."

Ms. Summer's story has all the ingredients: Mahalia Jackson was the role model, her father was the mentor, and her dream was to be a great and popular singer—a goal she has accomplished handsomely.

Mentors: mothers and others

Mentors can turn up almost anywhere all through our lives, provided they believe in us and actively help, coach, and encourage us in whatever the endeavor may be. The survey mothers spoke of scoutmasters, music teachers, and others as mentors for their achievers. One mother of a prominent scientist remembered her son's biology and chemistry professors. Another said her boy had "been in contact with persons of great capacities and influence who became interested in helping and furthering his development." Many spoke of fathers and older brothers and sisters as being important in leading the way and working with the child, getting him started on the long path to achievement. But just as with role models, mothers were the first mentors for many of the children, instilling the conviction they could succeed, and in many cases showing them how.

Mother—mentor and role model number one: Who was she?

Our data suggested that though the survey mothers came from a variety of backgrounds and experiences, they had something else in common besides raising achievers. They tended to be strong, colorful personalities. They had definite interests and firm beliefs. They lived their lives fairly decisively, having thought a great deal about what they were doing. Some had to run families entirely on their own, and they did so with admirable self-reliance. They appeared to be highly individualistic, and relatively unintimidated by what the neighbors thought—not only for themselves, but for their children.

But how do we mesh the figure of this strong, colorful individual with the "gifted mother" so carefully nourishing her children and their gifts a few chapters back? By recognizing that she not only nurtures, but also inspires and teaches—with words, and *by example*. We spoke with some of the mothers to see how, apart from their child-rearing techniques, they taught their children merely by being who they were. It was almost immediately apparent that they offered at least as much, if not more, in this way.

Ehrma Filer, mother of the chairman of Aetna Casualty: She recalls having been raised with a sense of "being special"; surrounded by books, she read voraciously. "I am still curious, and constantly looking things up in my dictionary." (She's eighty-five.) Her father wanted his daughters raised "so that they could earn a living if they needed to. My parents were very far-sighted. Although my friends thought it was crazy for a girl to go to college, I loved it." She gave up a successful teaching career to raise her children, but never gave up her interest in the outside world. "I always did three things, but not more: You have to narrow your interests somewhat. I always did church work—taught Sunday school; then there must be something for your town, like the Visiting Nurses or your school; then I was active in the Garden Club, just for fun." All this was part of a balanced life that pivoted on "the consistent effort to give much time to my children." Her child-rearing days may be past, but the spirit that sustained them certainly isn't: "I am fiercely independent—people don't understand it." And "If you think that at eighty you can't make new friends, you're crazy. You can't just let things go by!"

Katharine Fryer, mother of scientist Sarah Fryer Leibowitz: She says she's no good at giving advice, but she's written several books, and is director of the Fryer Research Center in New York. She wears pantsuits for comfort and flowers in her hair for style. She was widowed when her children were still in their teens. Shortly thereafter, her daughter Sarah went alone to Europe to study music. "I never worried about her—she was a very resourceful person. After a while, she couldn't bear to stay in her room and practice with all of Europe at her door, so she took the money and traveled. I could certainly understand that, couldn't you?" About women's liberation: "I'm very happy to be a woman. I wouldn't swap with any man. I was delighted to bear children, and was always blissfully happy to be pregnant. I always thought it was nice to have men help me, to lift things for me...the little amenities. But equal pay and opportunities for women? Of course....I dress in men's clothes, as you can see. I always do. It's more comfortable. But I decorate myself like a *woman.*"

Adele Ginzberg, mother of economist Eli Ginzberg, widow of renowned Jewish scholar, author, and theologian Louis Ginzberg, recalls being called "the American" as a girl back in Germany because she was "outspoken and modern"—years before she'd ever been to this country. Having been brought up in the strictest German fashion, she always said, "My revenge will come when I have children—I let them do everything, and I don't think I ever hit a child. I never had a governess or a nurse for my children although I was very busy with...many organizations."

When the whole family would pack into their cabin at a lake in Maine, she would get up at five to play tennis with instructors from a next-door camp; she taught her children and grandchildren to swim and fish. Even today she keeps up contacts at the Jewish Theological Seminary and with the grandchildren of her husband's colleagues. "I take one little credit for myself: namely, I love life. I have been active all these years, and even today, at ninety-three, I haven't slowed down—thanks to God's grace, which made me a strong person!" Friends suggested that she counsel the elderly: "When they have everything done for them, they turn into vegetables—I would get them going!"

All the mothers were impressive in their spirit and enthusiasm, and many more than these three have had active careers: Updike's mother, Linda Grace Hoyer, is a published novelist and short-story writer; Marjorie Guthrie is a teacher and founder of the Committee to Combat Huntington's Disease, which felled her husband. The committee is now active worldwide. The mothers of Maynard Jackson, Atlanta's mayor, and Barbara Newell, president of Wellesley, and Filia Holtzman were all college professors. Marietta Tree is now an international urban planner, having started that career in midlife: "I got absolutely fascinated with city planning...took nine courses in one year." Burt Bacharach's mother has studied art and painted for years. All of them downplayed their achievements, waving them aside as unimportant. They seemed more interested in other people, and in getting the job done, than in discussing their own accomplishments, which they briskly continued to pursue. They obviously were wonderful examples to their children, eloquent statements that they could grow to be what they wanted to be, too.

- *Who mentored the mentors?* Mentoring is like mothering: It helps if you've experienced it yourself. Several of the mothers spoke of their relationships with their own mothers as important in their child rearing. We've described Mrs. Gibson's thought that the warmth and respect she and her husband shared with their mothers was an example to her own boys. Katharine Fryer said "You see your mother do it successfully and you do it, too." Hers was "a celebrated opera singer at the Metropolitan for thirty years while raising six children....I don't remember feeling deprived at all. I never thought about it much, but she must have been a model for me."

Marietta Tree agreed that her relationship with her own very independent mother, a lifelong activist (arrested and jailed at the age of seventy-four in a civil rights demonstration) has affected her. She smiled when she said, "One always tries to do things differently from one's mother, but then unconsciously does the same thing." And achiever and mother Rosalyn Yalow, pointing out that she and her husband each want to raise their children as they were raised, said, "We all tend to duplicate our childhoods—if they were good, by replicating them; if they were bad, by doing the opposite." She speculated that, in any case, "How much of what we do as parents is actually thought out?"

9. Education is a full-time adventure

In *The Little Darlings*, her history of how children were raised in America, Mary Cable says that "According to *The Parent's Monitor and Young People's Friend*, one of the many parents' magazines that began to appear after 1830, education meant the implanting of right dispositions, the cultivation of the heart, the guidance of the temper, the formation of character. It was not for a generation or two later that the word education came to mean primarily what one learned in school."

Now here we are in the 1980s, after half a century's reliance on experts, back to where the prevailing view of educators is that an individual's education is the totality of his experience: All dimensions of life contribute to it.

The survey mothers saw education both ways. On the one hand, the way they lived clearly demonstrates that they held the old- (and new-) fashioned view of education—

everything was seen to be part of it. On the other, they stressed academic success as absolutely vital to their children's future. Here their expectations of excellence really took form. As Joe Lieberman told us, "Doing average was never good enough."

Many mothers cited education when asked what they thought had been the critical influence on their youngster's success. "Desire for knowledge," was how HHS Secretary Patricia Harris's mother put it. "He has told us that we conveyed to him that knowledge was available to him just for the taking," said the mother of scientist Joel Cohen. "Education," wrote Senator Moynihan's mother simply. A celebrated writer's mother felt her greatest contribution to her child's success was "making it possible for her to attend college"; and another said she would have liked to spend more time with her children, but "it was necessary that I work in order that they continue their education."

This love of learning and willingness to sacrifice for it is not unusual among achievers. Drs. Mildred and Victor Goertzel studied the biographies of four hundred famous people such as Clara Barton, Albert Einstein, Pearl Buck, George Patton, and Pablo Casals, and found that 90 percent came from homes where learning and academic achievement were respected and encouraged. In a study of achievers in science, Dr. Ann Roe discovered that their parents, too, had shared a high regard for intellectual accomplishment and had valued learning as an end in itself.

One might have assumed such high esteem for education among better-off and better-educated parents, but its appearance across all the socioeconomic levels in the survey group was notable, even for a time when education was the great American dream route to success. (Remember Faye Dunaway's memory of her mother's belief in the dream, and being the first in her family to attain college?)

In managing their children's education—in all areas of life—for achievement, the survey parents thus played a dual role: They provided a continuously stimulating home environment, and they formed an active educational partnership with the schools.

Built-in components of a stimulating home life

Many parents who agree that stimulation is important for young children feel their job is done as soon as kids start school and teacher takes over. The survey parents, if anything, redoubled their involvement as their children grew.

We've already noted some of the nonschool influences the mothers felt contributed to their children's education: the high-level dinner table conversations covering politics, literature, science, world events; early exposure to cultural and artistic events; vacations, travel, and jobs; and the parade of guests who brought new ideas into the house and provided an opportunity for the children to learn to be at ease socially.

John Updike's mother, among others, thought being in a neighborhood where academic skill was highly valued had helped: "His schoolmates were very bright and competitive, with parents who were, for the most part, bright and competitive too." Irene Jackson, mother of Atlanta's mayor, and Marietta Tree both spoke of maintaining high standards of speech at home. This is an even greater challenge today, when countless errors are written into television ads to make them more catchy, and more are perpetrated daily by politicians and others misusing the language for all to hear and imitate. Mrs. Jackson felt her persistence ultimately helped her son in his work as an attorney, and Mrs. Tree believed her children were well-spoken not only because articulate conversation prevailed in their household, but because they had never been spoken down to. The adults spoke as adults and the children soon learned to keep up. We noted several other built-in components to this domestic educational environment in the survey families.

- *Variety of parental interests* Knowing that parents are the chief role models tells us right away that their interests—what they bring into the house in the way of magazines, papers, books; what they play at, talk about, and hang on the walls—all will have an effect on the children. Among the survey families, the range presented was impressive: music, art, sports, politics, crafts, business, science, furthering their own educations, volunteer and church work, gardening, travel, reading on every topic. Of course not every family did every thing but most did several; the variety offered to the survey children as a group was considerable.

- *Outside lessons* The survey parents also offered many options to their children. The array of lessons taken by the achievers dramatizes this: music, sports, religious instruction, dance, foreign language, private tutors, acting, baton, fishing, flying, composition, art, sculpture, speech. When it came to choosing outside lessons the parents usually gave freedom to the child—including freedom to change. Judith Jamison's mother remembered one of her contributions to her daughter as "giving her the opportunity to explore many areas"; and we've seen other examples such as the boy who took violin lessons but wound up an artist, and the girl who switched to science.

  Though most of the families lived in urban or suburban areas, those who lived in rural areas were just as determined, often driving many miles to lessons and back.

- *Hobbies* Most of the survey children also engaged in leisure learning pastimes at some point: 60 percent had hobbies; 40 percent had collections. Again the range was wide, including scouting; model building; working on mathematical puzzles; scientific experiments; studying or collecting animals, antiques, birds, coins, stamps, electric trains. These activities, when added to the outside lessons, show the remarkable breadth of the children's interests and involvement in their nonschool education.

Obviously children are affected by their geographical and financial circumstances. It's hard for a youngster from the Plains to get much sailing experience, or for an inner-city child to drive a tractor or ride a horse. It's much easier to practice and be perfect if the tennis court's in the backyard or the piano in the living room. Nevertheless, the survey mothers were able to tap a broad range of materials and experiences for their children, regardless of income or education, as anyone can. There's an ever-increasing pool of resources made up of children's museums, art centers, enrichment programs, and the like for parents to take advantage of. The key for parents is to be aware of the value of these various kinds of stimulation, and try to keep exposing their children to such active experiences rather than the passive ones of television or movies.

Overcoming the seductions of television

Now that we've told you how wonderful the survey mothers were as mediators of the environment and culture bearers, we must admit they had the field pretty much to themselves. Your rival—television—hadn't arrived for most of them. However captivating radio was, parents and children could still sit together and sew, work on stamp collections, or build models while it was on. Even so, when it came to radio (and TV for the younger achievers) the survey parents seem to have been fairly strict. One achiever, now a noted author, gave this some credit for her early inclination to books and writing: "Not having any distractions, not having television until after I was ten, and then only permitted an hour a night...I also had several friends who were very bookish too." Two-thirds said that when their children were small they spent fewer than five hours a week listening to the radio or watching TV. Only four children out of the entire sample devoted as much as ten to twenty hours a week to these media; and of those, only one spent more than twenty hours a week with a radio or TV set.

Compare this to recent A. C. Nielsen figures showing that children aged two to five now watch thirty-three hours of TV per week (nearly five hours a day); six- to eleven-year-olds, twenty-nine hours; twelve- to seventeen-year-olds, twenty-four hours. For grownups, there's a Washington *Post* poll of not long ago which showed that the average person eighteen or older watches three hours of TV every weekday and almost three and a half hours each Saturday and Sunday—twenty-two hours a week for most people. So in most homes, what with work and school and eating and sleeping and marketing and cooking, there isn't much time left for stimulating personal or family life.

Stimulation is designed to produce activity, a response, to get the wheels going. Passivity, the opposite of activity, is the archenemy of learning, and TV is probably the most passivity-inducing device we have short of deep sleep. However, sometimes the mind—as well as the eyes and ears—is engaged by things on TV. That's where parents come in.

The biggest challenge of handling TV in child rearing is, again, example. TV is at least as seductive to adults as it is to children. In millions of homes every evening, parents whose children may have questions about homework, or emotional, social, or academic problems to hash out never hear about them *because they don't want to be interrupted while watching TV.* And if Junior's watching, he doesn't want to stop either. Just as Mother and Dad feel they've worked all day long and are entitled to some rest and relaxation, he feels he's worked all day at school and should get to play too; homework seems an unfair burden. Especially if he's locked up with homework while Mom and Dad are roaring away at some mindless TV joke in the next room.

The solution? The most obvious is to give the TV away. But there are some valuable and wonderful things on TV that make the medium a magnificent boon to those of us who could never afford opera or ballet tickets, even if we did live in the big cities where they play. Or who would probably never get around to reading Thomas Hardy or Willa Cather, or who aren't likely to get a guided tour of an insect's eyeball or have Katharine Hepburn, Isaac Asimov, or Don Rickles over for tea.

The next best thing is to put the TV in a less available place, where it'll be a little harder to get to. And then, start using it positively.

- *Using TV positively* The basics are: (1) restrict the hours of TV watching; (2) use discrimination in what is watched; and (3) best of all, provide a more attractive alternative: yourself. Your interested, involved, caring self.

If your children are small, don't use TV as a babysitter. Watch a few shows yourself some Saturday morning and see how you feel about a steady four or five hours of it. Remember that when the TV goes on, your young child's whole independent fantasy life goes off. When you ask him about a problem later, he'll give you an answer he saw on TV, not one he figured out for himself. A youngster's imagination is directly proportional to his reading achievement, vocabulary scores, IQ tests, and so on. And they all relate to his later achievement. Give him challenging toys and try to spend more time with him yourself.

If your children are older, let the family confer and select shows of value they can watch together; then use them as a springboard for discussion. If it's a show or series like *Roots*, which many children were assigned by schools to watch, make sure your children understand the difference between fiction and fact. It's recently been found that millions of children believe these docudramas are reenactments of actual events rather than entertainment that is "grounded in fact." Nevertheless, such shows, as well as cultural and sports events, are meaty sources for family conversation and controversy.

Making your home a learning place

To help you find your way out of this dilemma, we consulted several experts for a few pointers on how you can reinforce your involvement and make your home a learning place in the TV era by bringing stimulation to your potential achievers. We spoke to educators Gloria Wolinsky and Judith Pasamanick at Hunter College and Columbia University, and Marianne Mossbach, a learning specialist who counsels parents and children at several schools in New York City.

Our experts gave a few general principles first. They explained that the old idea of education was that there was only one right answer. The youngster who repeated back the lesson most accurately got the *A*, and the *A* got the praise. Other ideas offered by the students weren't even discussed. Soon the children—and their parents—became oriented toward marks as the major, if not only, goal of education.

- *Learning is discovery* Now the idea is that to learn is to find out, to acquire and use knowledge for its own purposes, not just to please teacher. This way the children develop a creative, problem-solving ability for more challenging tasks. Teachers now try to provide learning experiences that involve an entire process so children can see how things connect, rather than merely memorizing isolated facts. If there are sugar maples in the school yard, the science teacher might have the youngsters do everything to make maple syrup: check the temperature, gather the sap, boil it down, and pack the syrup. Thus they learn about weather, tree physiology, physical properties of ingredients at different temperatures, and they end up with a treat for the family, which will elicit the kind of reinforcement that motivates for the next project or task.

- *Reading is the big payoff* Reading, said the experts, is the most valuable key to future success. By becoming easy and fluent in the language, a person—as a child or at any age—is free to find out things for himself. He no longer has to depend on what others—parents, teachers, TV reporters, other kids in the street—tell him. Whatever you do to make your youngster comfortable with words, language, literature, speaking, writing, and/or singing will benefit his future creative freedom and adaptability.

We already know that nearly every one of the survey parents read to their children from babyhood on. Nearly 40 percent had 200 or more books on their shelves (parents of the science/scholarship group had the largest libraries). About 30 percent had between 50 and 200, and the rest had under 50 books, mostly because they couldn't afford more. Many of these, as did others, said they were enthusiastic library visitors, some going as often as two or three times a week.

How can you help at home? With these two ideas in mind, of learning as exploring and reading as the payoff, we asked for specific tips to help today's mothers of preschool as well as school-age youngsters maximize their children's educational experience at home.

1. *Be aware that your home is already a learning place.* Many parents teach their children spontaneously without being aware of it, functioning very much the same way as creative teachers. Though you may not be a teacher and the nearest sugar maple might be a thousand miles away, there's sure to be something in your region that can be grown, harvested, and pickled, canned, frozen, or otherwise turned into a delicious treat. Small children helping their mothers cook will see the size of the measuring cup or cooking pot selected, the quantities of ingredients, and their properties as they are mixed and baked. We don't think of these as exercises in spatial relationships or chemistry, but they can be. Think of making ice or ice cream (crystalliza-

tion) or even frying pancakes (heat makes the butter soften, the batter harden). Making a shopping list is practice in planning and writing for an older child. Handling increasing amounts of money helps teach math and accounting. Many complex concepts, such as numerical sequences or time measurement, grow out of a gradual understanding of relationships which a parent interprets for a child over a period of time.

  2. *Let nature take its course.* Studies show that children advance at their own pace. Don't be eager to have the first reader or writer on the block. Just make a few toys and materials available to your child, and he will use them when he's ready. In fact, formal learning procedures and drills at too early an age can be negative for some youngsters, because they'll be struggling for one thing only—the smile or cookie they get for giving you the right answer. It may be almost impossible for them to unlearn this habit of seeking praise rather than self-satisfaction as the end of learning. A number of mothers also warned of rushing their children ahead of their natural schedule. One said, when asked what she'd do over, "Feed him on a demand schedule and not be in such a hurry for him to lose his babyhood. He was a precocious child and I think we sometimes expected too much of him."

  3. *Invest in the payoff: reading.* Start reading to your youngster when he's still an infant, and never stop. As he gets older, work up to more complex material, even if he's already reading on his own. Let your youngster into your reading world too. When he's very young, go through your newspaper with him, showing him the pictures and explaining. When he's a bit older, introduce him to the national weather map in the paper and ask him what the temperature was in some distant city yesterday. Don't read watered-down versions of the classics—the real ones should be part of his experience, so he will be exposed to other ways of saying things, different from his everyday language.

Read to the child's interests: If he's crazy about dinosaurs, or horses, or bugs, give him everything you've got on it, not just kiddie books. Ignore his reading level—children don't have to understand every word. Quickly define the tough ones as you go along, or show him how to use the dictionary. Giving him access to more than one book lets him know there are many approaches to the same subject, and suggests that he might even have something to add. When your children are old enough, introduce them to the local library and get them library cards of their own; show them how to use the many library services and other local sources for finding things out: museums, state offices, historical societies, and so on.

Finally, reading is always something you can share. If you're reading something that moves you, share it with your youngster as a gift you share with someone you care for. Share the emotions the book or article evokes, and be honest about it—not all learning is enjoyable.

4. *Expose the child to experiences at his interest level.* A very young child will see or hear something and ask about it. This is an opportunity to extend from his interest to teach him something: "Yes, a baby cat is called a kitten. What do kittens eat?" Or, "Yes, that is a truck. What are they carrying in the back?" In this way, a child is encouraged to use words and formulate ideas.

For older children, sitting down together at meals and discussing topics they can share in automatically involves them in the adventure of learning. It defuses the "schoolish" aspect: Learning becomes simply the fun of satisfying curiosity and sharing news with others. For instance, if you assign everyone, including yourself, to bring a fact a night to the dinner table, you'll find this can lead to some pretty lively conversations. Further, whether you're discussing an item you clipped from the morning paper or something they learned in biology, your children will get the message that everything they learn about was either invented by or happened to an ordinary person just like those around the dinner table, instead of to some lifeless name in a book. Children who learn to participate this way bring well-developed intellectual and verbal muscles to the challenges facing them as they mature.

5. *Expose the child to experiences on your interest level.* Just as the survey mothers did, let your enthusiasms spill over into your child's life: Bring home souvenirs, theater programs, menus from unusual restaurants, maps from trips. Tell the youngster what you did and didn't enjoy, and give details of your adventures. Take him to museums, concerts, exhibitions, and cultural events that interest you. You can start this as early as you like, even carrying your baby in a backpack.

6. *Make learning a game.* The earlier you share things with children in a light and playful way, the more you preempt the imprint that "learning is work, learning is hard, learning happens at school." There are dozens of ways learning can be made into a game or something fun if *you* make it fun. Remember, the child takes his lead from you. Play word games, have spelling bees, organize family outings around school projects (visit historical sites, the zoo, the aquarium), or even—with a very young child—use things like the growing-harvesting-canning process we've mentioned or any cooking adventure.

7. *Reinforce accomplishments and praise selectively.* Here you're accentuating the positive in the educational setting. When your child brings home artwork or a good term paper, be specific about what you're reacting to. If you especially like the way he or she used texture in the painting, or an idea in the paper, say so. It's always gratifying when we know the person we're talking to is really listening or seeing. The emphasis on detail also stimulates the child to think about what and how he is doing something. In this way, you can continually reinforce the child's progress and his standards.

9. *Give the youngster his own turf.* Even a very young child needs a place for his possessions, a bit of wall for

his pictures or cards. This is especially important if there are many children in the family. Even if this is only an enclosure of screens, or a box and a bulletin board, or a set of shelves, it creates a sense of "my own place" which gives the child the feeling that he has an identity others recognize and respect. This comes up in counseling sessions frequently. Recently one mother, seeking help for a troubled child (her sixth), was startled to realize he was the only one in the family who had never been assigned a definite place at the dinner table. Another mother was amused and touched when her son asked if she would mail him a greeting card. "For what occasion?" she asked. "No occasion," came the reply. "I'd just like to receive a greeting card." When the card arrived, the little boy opened the card joyfully and taped it over his desk, where it stayed for many months.

As a child gets older, parents can cultivate this sense of identity in other ways: buying the child a camera to record his impressions, letting him plan a parent's birthday dinner, and so on.

9. *Leave free, unscheduled time for the child.* Children need time to play and be by themselves. Don't schedule every free minute with some educational or other activity for your youngster, even if he or she begs for ballet on Monday, tennis on Tuesday, riding on Wednesday, and so on. Many observers deplore that adolescents, and even younger children, are caught up in the national productivity compulsion, where every hour must be put to constructive purpose. When we see children dreaming or at play, we're often guilty of pressuring them to do their homework, practice the piano, or pick up their rooms, often because *we* would feel a greater sense of accomplishment if they did. Responding to our cues, they begin to feel vaguely guilty when they relax. We should remember that while the source of this compulsion may be the Protestant work ethic, that same religious system was equally rigid about enforcing a day of rest, recognizing that it was mandatory for survival.

Many creative individuals have discovered their creativity in empty times of solitude. Sensitivity to a child's need for this kind of open, exploring time leads parents to keep room for it too.

The educational partnership: school and you

Most of the survey group were educated in public schools from first grade; a few attended private schools some or all of the time. Either way, teachers agree that the school and the parents make up a partnership. This works best when there is two-way communication, so that when things aren't working out for the child, the parents feel free to voice concerns and push for new solutions at school, just as the teacher has always addressed his concerns to parents. Here are some tips to help you live up to your side of the partnership.

1. *Know what is going on—or supposed to be going on—in the classroom.* Being familiar with curriculum has many advantages. You can identify problem areas, for one. If you know the subject matter doesn't turn off your child but the class does, you can work on the personality clash with the teacher, difficulty in getting to the lab, or whatever the obstruction is. You can also sense if things are going the other way—your child just skimming through without being challenged. Mrs. Filer, who'd been a schoolteacher, realized her son was getting all *A*'s simply by memorizing his work but that he wasn't retaining any of it. To the boy's chagrin, she insisted he be moved: "I said this child must be put under stricter teachers. He needs to be worked harder. ...Well, they put him under stricter teachers and he learned.... You have to do that in public schools; the education is there, but you have to check it, or you get through with a very minor education."

Moral and ethical considerations also come up in discussing school subjects with your child. You might feel disturbed, as many parents do, to find that textbooks or course material sometimes don't give the full picture: that the settlement of the western states, the Civil or Second World Wars can all be studied without any discussion of the dispersal of the Indians, the abuses of slavery, or the massacre of the Jews. You can provide a different slant on such topics without fear of interfering with education, but with a view to taking responsibility for your share in it. If you take a "there are many viewpoints" attitude rather than a challenging one ("Who's right—me or the teacher?"), your child will learn that he too is entitled to an opinion; his self-reliance will be reinforced.

2. *Be prepared to give some of your time to his schoolwork.* We tend to bring our own feelings about school to this situation. Often, our remembered reluctance to do homework assignments when we were schoolchildren leads us to pressure our children rather than help them.

Constant nagging to "get your homework done" can decrease a child's motivation, but many parents find that if they sit with a child briefly to check on his problems, they can get him over the first hurdle. For instance, you may remember that the information he needs is in a book on your own shelf, or help him conceptualize the essay he's to write. He'll carry on from there. It's your love and attention that make him feel it's worth it.

This kind of support is important and has a lasting effect. Many of the achieving children remembered their parents helping them with homework. The most striking account came from the Barany boys. They felt they owed to their mother not only their scholarly accomplishments, but their whole feeling for knowledge itself. As one said:

She created the atmosphere; she has the understanding of what motivates an intellectual. This is something I share with her to this day. It wasn't just that she was dedicated to the family; she got into the material and presented it dynamically. She taught me algebra as a game, not even labeling it as such. She also made a point of teaching things to supplement the curriculum. She introduced us to Shakespeare through the Charles Lamb stories; our introduction to opera was through synopses, and she progressed through them, starting with the most tuneful and appealing. Everything was carefully thought out. Our time alone together was spent communicating.

3. *Balance the emphasis on marks with positive talk of other attributes.* Everyone has met the mother whose first words after "How do you do" are of her child's high test scores and class standing. Whenever she introduces him, she talks only about this; he in turn has nothing to say of himself or of his hopes and dreams. He is tense and preoccupied with fears of failure because, quite naturally, his whole identity—and his mother's love—seem to rest on his school success. He may be ahead of his class now, but chances are that—thanks to his stage mother—he has much tougher lessons ahead in life.

Many educational systems have used competition as a motivator, from the class standings to the early-college-admission system. Law and medical students are famous victims of the tensions of competition, but you can see disturbing evidence of it even at grade-school age. To help your children get the proper perspective as well as avoid the competitive rat race that so many institutions promote, discuss the long-range values of good moral character and other nonacademic abilities to emphasize that *everyone*— even those at the bottom of the class—has something important to contribute.

For one thing, those at the bottom may not belong there. Children whose first language is not fluent English often cannot perform up to their true levels on tests of verbal ability. Second, most of us learn in our adult lives that success usually has more to do with ability to handle people, individually and in groups, than it does with intellectual quickness. Finally, creativity may also be more important to performance than grades. Psychologist Calvin Taylor measured on-the-job performance of a group of practicing physicians and then attempted to correlate it to their college and medical school grades. This revealed something many of us have often suspected: Grades showed no significant relationship to performance for 97 percent of the sample.

Even for the remaining 3 percent, most of the correlations were negative. That is, physicians performing better in practice had *lower* grades in school. When Taylor studied scientists, undergraduate grade averages again failed to correlate with ultimate success. Instead, more personal undertakings, such as participation in summer science programs as a high school student, were better indicators of the creative adult scientist than classroom grades. Several of the survey mothers might agree. Mothers of scientific achievers remarked on such influences, as did the mother of a noted artist. She recalled that her son had received a summer scholarship to art school which had changed his whole life."

4. *Keep the alliance going with your child.* We've described the problem-solving alliance with children, whereby even if the problem *is* the child, parents convey that they are working with him rather than against him. This becomes more important as children get older and feel the generation gap widening. Parents and teachers seem to join in a solid wall of authority, just when children want parental support more than ever in their wars with the educational establishment. Ideally parents, teachers, and the child are a team; if parents are able to convince the child they are on his side—even if they aren't going to do exactly what he wants—the team will have a much better chance of success.

The survey parents had many conferences with teachers and administrators; often, as in Mrs. Filer's case, they found that their aims were different or more demanding than the school's. One mother spoke of "how different the school seemed from the home." Parents who weren't requesting that children skip grades, change rooms or teachers might be arguing against skipping when recommended by the school; other times they fought for their teenagers whose talents lay outside the academic sphere. There was never any doubt that the child's interest was the top priority. Some of the mothers taking a forceful position in school situations had been teachers themselves, so they were less awed by the system than others might have been. Many of us retain into adulthood our early image of school authority, especially if it was backed by parental admonitions that teacher knows best. In fact, teacher's often at a loss; the mothers who had themselves taught knew this, and we can take a cue from them: The clearer the picture both parents and teachers have of the child, the better they will be able to form a supporting alliance—even if the child's embarrassed by it, which he probably will be.

Problems at school

A number of the survey parents, despite all their love and concern and talent for child rearing, remembered having problems. A common difficulty with older children was their becoming consumed by a single interest, or by interests outside school. A budding physicist may thrill his science teachers, but the French teacher may not be impressed if it means he's slipping behind in irregular verbs. Burt Bacharach's mother said, "My major problem was his lack of interest in school, and in reaching the realization that music was all-important to him." Once this happened, about the only other thing that mattered to her son was that "sports were still an important part of his life," which wasn't much help in the academic world either. In fact, for many of the achievers in arts and entertainment, formal learning was a poor second precisely because their burning interest could only be expressed outside school doors and hours. A noted author, however, was described as having "interests so varied he did not concentrate on one enough to excel until later on." This same trait is now of value in a career which involves writing about a variety of subjects.

The mothers also reported that 10 percent of the children had speech problems, 10 percent had reading difficulties, and two of the children were just plain "difficult in general." Others had periodic rough spots: one mother reported that her son's rebelliousness started around sixth grade and continued off and on through college. His academic record showed marked ups and downs, so she sought professional consultation and tried changing schools. She acknowledged being angry and disappointed at times, but always showed she loved him and gave strong sympathetic support when he was upset or depressed, as well as encouraging his efforts to be more responsible.

In education, then, as in everything else, the mothers of achievers were reconfirming their original commitment. Providing varied stimulation at home and establishing a working relationship at school were important ways of expressing their high expectations, belief in the child's future, intense involvement, encouragement of gifts, and their solid emotional support for the emerging adult.

10. Bringing up achievers in single-parent and working-mother households

The survey data suggested strongly that the intactness of the families was a positive factor in raising achievers, since no less than 84 percent of them came from families where both parents were in place throughout the child-rearing period; mother was usually at home when the children were young, too.

    Today this is much less likely to be true. Already one child in six lives in a single-parent home, and as the divorce rate passes 50 percent, that figure is likely to increase. One child in two is in a home where both parents work. Many are in homes with a single parent who also works: Of the 9 million single-parent homes, most (7.5 million) are headed by mothers, most of whom hold full-time jobs; this is even more likely to be true of the 1.5 million households headed by fathers.

Since there are still going to be bank presidents, senators, scientists and artists among us, this means a good many of tomorrow's achievers will come from such homes. Though the 16 percent of the survey achievers from single-parent homes was well below today's average, this may be at least partly explained by the fact that it was a period when divorce was far less acceptable than it is now. Much more interesting is that the number of working mothers in the sample was almost as high as it would be today. Close to 60 percent of the mothers worked at some time, more than a few when their children were very small. More than a third of these worked forty or more hours a week, most of the rest between twenty and forty hours a week.

In some cases, these circumstances were a matter of parental choice—divorce or separation, or just wanting to work; other times illness, death, or financial shortages had brought them about.

We're not saying being a single parent is the same as being a working mother with a spouse. There's no question that it's easier to raise children with a cooperating parent on hand, working or not, than without one. Being able to share decisions, problems, and the emotional load, as well as financial and caretaking duties, makes a considerable difference. As one of the survey mothers, divorced when her daughter was three, said in answer to the "what was your major problem in raising your child" question: "None—except for myself, having to make all decisions alone." We have put single-parenting and working motherhood together here because the child-rearing situations are comparable, and the solutions and suggestions we've gathered from the survey mothers and other sources are applicable to both.

Stability, harmony, and intactness

Though our research relates stability to intactness, the survey mothers who had to do it alone showed that it's possible to create stability without both parents being in place or, in the case of working mothers, with both parents as part of a household but not in it much of the time. The key to stability is not the fact of staying together or staying at home so much as it is creating a family environment that is stable, that gives the child a feeling of warmth and security, of something he or she can depend on.

An equally important factor in raising achievers is harmony at home. Clearly, divorcing parents are choosing harmony over intactness. Unlike previous decades, it's now accepted that there is no point in staying together "for the children" if it's going to mean years of suffering and tension for the whole family. The negative effects on youngsters may be far greater than those that would result from separating in order to achieve harmony. We'd expect divorced parents to endorse this view, but it is more interesting to note that many teenagers of divorced parents have indicated that they also preferred it that way.

Working mothers, like divorcing parents, must also tussle with priority conflicts. Mother may fret about leaving her children, especially if they're young, but her extra income may relieve financial stress which is causing more serious problems. If she's bored and restless as a stay-at-home, she can unwittingly create such pressure in the family circle that the advantages of her going to work would far outweigh those of her staying home.

One positive aspect of the changing marital family structure, if there can be said to be one, is that children of divorce and other single-parent homes are better off socially than they were in years past, when such things were whispered about and swept under the carpet. No one makes a fuss anymore, and such children are no longer forced to feel strange or unaccepted if mother isn't waiting at the kitchen door with milk and cookies when they get home from school. This is a very important change. Feelings of self-esteem are closely related to the need to achieve. In the past, studies have shown a correlation between children of divorce and low achievement as adults, just as—from the same era—there's the correlation we've noted between family stability and high achievement.

Furthermore, children's needs are now top priority among responsible divorcing adults, the courts, schools, and communities. Great expense in both time and money has gone into learning the problems facing children of divorce and how best to overcome them, employing everything from achievement programs to special textbooks to counseling for the whole family.

Tips for raising achievers

Despite today's unsettled domestic scene, the message of the survey data was that the right attitudes and approaches paid off equally well in single-parent as well as two-parent homes. However, we did find a few specifics that may help you in raising achievers in single-parent and working-mother households today:

1. *Don't be afraid to wear both hats.* We spoke to Professor Stephen Dworkin, who has studied and lectured on the changing roles of parents. He said that historically, mothers created the feeling in the child that he or she is "internally safe" through nurturing, physical comfort, and warmth; while fathers produced a feeling of being "externally safe" through breadwinning and organizing the security of the family. Dworkin feels that, actually, many women are excellent at the external-security functions and many men at the internal ones. We've already mentioned the many breadwinner mothers; and though some divorced fathers who have custody of their children hire child-care

help, others—especially those able to work at home—do it themselves and find they are very good at it.

Dworkin is impressed with "the adaptability of the sexes, the androgyny within us all," and even questions the current axiom that children really need role models of both sexes. Perhaps, he thinks, they can identify with both male and female aspects of a parent who is performing all roles, especially if he or she is doing it so capably the child feels loved, stimulated, and secure. There's no conclusive research on this notion, but it's Dworkin's contention that if this weren't the case, "the millions of children being raised in one-parent homes would have more problems in this area than they seem to."

2. *Sustain the commitment.* There is concern, however, over the situation of "two parents in a home where *neither* is oriented to the children." Whether such parents happen to be married, separated, or divorced is far less important than "their need to farm out the children, and many children are now being cared for by third parties.... So many people don't like to be parents; this is the frightening thing."

Dworkin has here put his finger on the key to raising achievers in one-parent and working-mother homes. The secret is simply sustaining the commitment to the child in such a way that the child knows it. Even when mother has had to be away from the children from an early age, if they are assured of her abiding love and care, and if she has provided someone stable and loving to watch over them in her absence, their chances of maintaining self-esteem are much greater.

3. *Delegate with care—don't farm out.* Among lower-income families in the survey, stand-ins for working mothers might be relatives, neighbors, or friends; in more affluent homes they would be housekeepers, maids, or nannies. Continuity was a feature in both cases. Many families had the same child-care figures throughout their children's youth, whether it was granny or a nanny. But this delegation

of their children's care to others in no way seemed to diminish the intensity of the mother's involvement.

If you're delegating child care to someone else, you can make efforts to insure that your child-care helpers are as good, or even better in some ways, than you might be if you were home. Search for the kind of person who doesn't just plop the youngsters in front of TV, but sees to their proper meals, fresh air, and exercise; as well as adding to their lives and experiences, such as by teaching them to knit or carve, or by reading to them. In other words, look for nurturing rather than the bare minimum of caretaking—that is, just seeing that they don't get into trouble or make too much noise.

4. *Maintain a positive attitude and make positive use of your job.* Even when mother is working because she must and not because she wants to, if her attitude is positive it's likely the effect will be as well. It's important that mothers enjoy their work as much as possible, so they can bring home positive impressions rather than make their youngsters feel a burden because it is on their account she's obliged to work. If you're a single mother or father holding down a job, your interest in the job and the fulfillment you get from it will serve as a positive example to your children.

You can also involve your children in your work and in this way expand their experience, as well as reassure them. More than other children, they need to know where you are and what you're doing when you're away from them and home. One advantage of being a working parent is that—unlike stay-at-home mothers who may be at the supermarket, department store, or neighbor's house—your kids know where you are: at work all day, just as they're in school. Use it. Take them to your office and show them what you do. Introduce them to your coworkers so you can chat about them later at home. Bring home things such as company publications or a piece of cake from an office party, and show that you sometimes have to do "homework" too.

Take their pictures and muffins they bake to work and tell them how your coworkers responded.

5. *Emphasize the quality of your time with your children instead of the quantity.* Working and single parents can't spend as much time with their children as they would like to, but we were interested to see that *nonworking* as well as working mothers from the survey remarked on this. These were some answers to the "How would you do it over?" question: "Have more time with my son—I'd spend less time on my own social activities"; "I would have seen more of them"; "I would try to be with them even more than I was."

But the evidence shows it's not really the amount of time spent with children but rather the richness of that time that counts. Remember the study of newborns that showed it wasn't the 65 percent of the time spent either by mothers in caretaking or in babies playing by themselves while mother was in the room that mattered. It was the 35 percent that the mother spent interacting with the babies that had the impact on the children's achievement. This attitude is well expressed by Sarah Leibowitz, a mother and full-time scientific researcher whose husband also works. In speaking of her children: "We enjoy them so much! We are so consumed, in time and energy, at our work, they are the other whole half of our lives...We spend our time with them when we're free, and they accept our life completely, even the traveling I sometimes have to do."

Parents who may have spent many hours a day under the same roof with their children, but who were reading magazines, talking to friends on the phone, watching TV or doing housecleaning projects are simply not going to have the same effect on their children as those who've had only one hour a day but have used it in direct involvement with the children. Nor are they going to have the same memories of their child-rearing years. These brief hours are your only opportunity to share conversation, ideas, worries and woes, laughter and love. This is where the children learn their values, and also how to raise their own children, whether or not they become single or working parents.

This doesn't mean that you should cram something "meaningful" into every second you're home with the child. It means that being involved with and aware of your youngster will be of inestimable value to both of you, now and in years to come.

6. *Make special efforts.* Most single and working parents do this anyway in one way or another, but we can take a tip from the survey mothers. Remember Mrs. Barany, calling her children from work every day just to say hello? And carefully setting aside a separate hour for each when she got home? Or Mrs. Gibson's saving a few precious minutes early in the morning to share with her boys? More than just making good use of rare time, this is making a special effort, and children recognize and appreciate it.

Make a big fuss over birthdays; be sure their Halloween costumes are special; pack super lunches and put notes in them. All are ways of telling your children you're thinking of them even when you're away from them, and could be much more attention than many stay-at-home mothers—who just toss the peanut butter and jelly into the lunchbox—take time for.

You can also add to their school and after-school life by leaving a note with an apple and cookie or other treat along with a game or partly started puzzle for them to complete by the time you get home. If they're younger, it would be building blocks or a coloring book. This not only helps avoid the TV syndrome, it also gives you something to talk about and praise them for when you arrive.

Get yourself a library card too. If you're working, you'll frequently be closer to a big downtown library with a wider choice of books and records than the neighborhood one, and you can expand their opportunities that way, showing you care at the same time.

Make a serious effort to attend school functions. Stay in close touch with teachers, at school and for music, sports, dancing, or other lessons. Again, use your advantages: Teachers and other professionals are working people too, many with children, and they often show consideration of this in dealing with working parents.

7. *Take the opportunity to let your children join the adult world early.* It is critical that every child enjoy a childhood free of too-heavy responsibilities for others, at least when young. But early self-reliance was a hallmark of the achievers, and children from single-parent homes have special opportunities for this, especially as they get older. Single parents often report amazement at how mature their children become when they share financial, work, vacation, and other plans with them. When there are two parents running a family, they tend to discuss these subjects with each other, forgetting that the children are able to comprehend, participate in, and offer useful input in these same issues.

In addition to these pointers, single and working parents can easily adapt the other ideas and techniques in this book into their life-styles. Being close to children, making the home a learning place, sharing ideals and values are certainly not limited to two-parent homes; they're a part of every family's life.

Ultimately, while there are definitely problems associated with child-rearing in single-parent or working-mother households, the survey showed us that if the positive point of view and feelings of loving care are in place in the home, the atmosphere is far more conducive to nurturing achievers—or any children—than in two-parent homes where these vital supports are missing.

11. Are you raising an achiever? Test yourself

Reading over the responses of the survey mothers and the information from the research on achievement makes us curious to see how we stack up as parents. What kind of parents are we? Are we doing the most we can to bring out all the potential in our children? To help them bring it out in themselves? We put together this small questionnaire based on the one we sent the mothers (a complete one is in the back of the book) so parents could see how they would answer. We updated it by adding a couple of questions about TV. Some of the questions refer to young (usually under twelve) children. If your children are young, answer accordingly; if they're a bit older, respond with what you remember about your children when they were younger. Most important, try to resist the urge to give "right" answers. The more honest you are, the more useful you'll find your answers will be. At the end of the questionnaire, we've summarized the responses from the mothers so you can compare notes with them.

Are you raising an achiever?

Reader's Questionnaire

1. Below are 10 activities and areas of interest. Check columns for *all* that appeal to, or interest, you and your spouse. Fill in the blank if your interests aren't on the list.

	Of interest to:	
	You	*Your Spouse*
a. Music, literature, painting, other artistic areas	( )	( )
b. Science (read science magazines, visited museums, used a telescope, microscope, etc.)	( )	( )
c. Business (concerned with job, career, or office; making money, investments, etc.)	( )	( )
d. Family (spent time with spouse and children; concerned with children's activities in school, etc.)	( )	( )
e. Sports and outdoor activities (as participant or fan)	( )	( )
f. Social (enjoyed being with friends for conversation, cards, to pass time of day; belonged to lodges, clubs)	( )	( )
g. Workshop, crafts, gardening (enjoyed making things around house)	( )	( )
h. Politics (took part in local or national politics; was an avid reader of current political events)	( )	( )
i. Furthering education (getting diploma or degree, other professional advancement)	( )	( )

	Of interest to:	
	You	Your Spouse

j. TV, radio (listening, watching, stereo/tape equipment, collection)   ( )   ( )

k. Other: _____   ( )   ( )

2. Which of the interests you checked is *most* important to you? _____ Next most important to you? _____ Most important to your spouse? _____ Next most important to him? _____

3. When you and your spouse take vacations, do you generally (check *one* response):

Take the children   ( )
Make other arrangements for the children   ( )
Rarely take vacations   ( )

4. If your child is young, (under twelve), how much emphasis do you place on the following (check *one* response for each item):

	Great deal	Some	Very little	None at all
a. Protecting him, worrying about his welfare	( )	( )	( )	( )
b. Providing strict discipline	( )	( )	( )	( )
c. Your being involved in his daily activities	( )	( )	( )	( )

5. Of the following choices, check the *two* you like best about small children (under twelve):

a. When they are neat and clean   ( )
b. When they hug and kiss you   ( )
c. Playing with them   ( )
d. When they do what you tell them to   ( )
e. When they're well-mannered with others   ( )
f. When they finally learn to do something after a long time ( )
g. When they play nicely with other children   ( )

6. At approximately what age do you expect your child to do the following things (*circle* the appropriate age):
a. To know his way around the neighborhood
   4 yrs.   5 yrs.   6 yrs.   7 yrs.   8 yrs.   9 or older
b. To hang up his own clothes and look after his own possessions
   4 yrs.   5 yrs.   6 yrs.   7 yrs.   8 yrs.   9 or older
c. To take part in his parents' interests
   4 yrs.   5 yrs.   6 yrs.   7 yrs.   8 yrs.   9 or older
d. To do homework by himself
   4 yrs.   5 yrs.   6 yrs.   7 yrs.   8 yrs.   9 or older
e. To buy something at the store alone
   4 yrs.   5 yrs.   6 yrs.   7 yrs.   8 yrs.   9 or older

7. If your child is young (under twelve), and fulfills your expectations, or is "good," how do you react? (Check *three* of these items.)
a. Give him a special treat or privilege ( )
b. Show him you expected it ( )
c. Kiss or hug him to show how pleased you are ( )
d. Show him how it could have been done even better ( )
e. Do nothing at all to make it seem special ( )
f. Tell him what a good child he is. Praise him for being good. ( )

8. If your child is young (under twelve), and misbehaves or disappoints you, how do you react? (Check *three* of these items.)
a. Show him you are disappointed in him ( )
b. Don't show any feelings about it ( )
c. Point out how he should have behaved ( )
d. Scold or spank him ( )
e. Deprive him of something he likes or wants ( )
f. Just wait until he does what you want ( )

9. Would you say that your family life is generally (check one):

Extremely turbulent and emotional	( )
Somewhat turbulent and emotional	( )
Somewhat calm and harmonious	( )
Extremely calm and harmonious	( )

10. How important do you think it is that your child grow up to (check *one* for each item):

	Very	Some-what	Not very	Not at all
a. Be a good person	( )	( )	( )	( )
b. Be independent	( )	( )	( )	( )
c. Be happy	( )	( )	( )	( )
d. Attain a standard of excellence or high achievement	( )	( )	( )	( )
e. Be well-liked	( )	( )	( )	( )

11. Of the following attributes or talents, which three do you most emphasize to your growing child? Which three do you think your spouse tries to emphasize? (Check *three* in each column).

	Emphasized by You	Your spouse
Education and learning	( )	( )
Musical ability	( )	( )
Athletic ability	( )	( )
Money and financial success	( )	( )
Getting along with others	( )	( )
Being religious	( )	( )
Family closeness	( )	( )
Interest in science	( )	( )
Interest in art	( )	( )
Interest in current events, politics	( )	( )
Other_____	( )	( )

Are you raising an achiever?

12. Do you ever read to your child? Yes____ No____ If yes, about how old was he when you began to read to him? ____ years old. When you stopped (if you have) reading to him? ____ years old. About how many times a week do you usually read to your child? (check *one*):
Every day ( ) At least once a week ( )
A few times a week ( ) Two or three times
  a month ( )

About how many books are available to him in your home (check *one*):
Under 50 ( ) Between 200 and 500 ( )
Between 50 and 200 ( ) Over 500 ( )

13. Does your child often listen to the radio or watch television? Yes____ No____ If yes, about how many hours a week? (check *one*):

	Radio	TV
Less than 5 hours	( )	( )
Between 5 and 10 hours	( )	( )
Between 10 and 20 hours	( )	( )
Over 20 hours	( )	( )

14. Has your child ever taken special lessons outside school (music, riding, dance, religious instruction, etc.)
Occasionally ( )   Often ( )   Never ( )

15. How often do you usually entertain at home?
More than once   Once a month ( )
a week ( )
Several times   Less than once
a month ( ) a month ( )

16. Do you devote time, on a regular basis, to a career, activities or other interests outside your home and family?
Yes ( )
Yes, but not regularly ( )
Never ( )

Now compare your answers to the ones we obtained from the mothers of our superstars:

- *Family closeness (1,2,3)* Sharing interests and being involved with each other help keep families close. Among the survey parents, there was considerable overlap in these listings (Question 1) for mother and father, indicating interests they were able to share over the years. They may have started out in life with quite different tastes, but if so, clearly one or both had adapted so their enthusiasms could be mutual.

    On the mothers' lists, the most frequently checked item was "family." All the women said that "spending time with spouse and children, being concerned with children's school activities," and similar family matters were of interest to them. "Family" was also chosen as most important (Question 2) by more mothers than any other item. Music, literature, and the arts came second; social was third. The fathers shared the same first two choices, followed by business and sports. We've included TV and radio on this questionnaire so you can make some judgments as to how big an interest it is in your life today.

    Question 3, about vacations, showed that 88 percent of the parents took their children with them, another sign of family closeness.

- *Involvement with children (4,5)* Parents of achievers tended to be enthusiastically involved with their children and less concerned with enforcing rules than with encouraging the children to be themselves. Responses to Question 4 showed that about 65 percent of the mothers said (a) mattered a "great deal," 55 percent said (c) did, both being choices showing emotion and involvement. Only about 20 percent gave this importance to (b), the item about discipline. Feelings about little children were also indicative of this (Question 5). Of the seven choices given, an emotional, involved one (b) was at the top of the mothers' list. At the bottom were (d) and (a), controlling, rule-enforcing choices.

Manners (e), which involves self-reliance as well as rules, was second choice; (c), (f), and (g)—two emotional choices and a "rules" choice, respectively, were tied for third.

- *Self-reliance (6,7,8)* Their attitude favoring self-reliance may have caused these parents to expect their children to do things unassisted sooner than other parents might have. Question 6 showed that over half the mothers expected their children to know their way around the neighborhood by age five; nearly half expected them to put away their own things by five, and take part in parents' interests by six; 60 percent expected them to do their homework or buy something at the store alone by the time they were seven.

  Two other expressions of this were their techniques of rewards and punishment, both operating to enhance the child's sense of self-worth. The survey mothers relied heavily on praise and demonstrations of pleasure and affection as rewards. Answering Question 7, 75 percent recalled praising their children (f); 61 percent showed approval with physical affection—hugs and kisses (c); 59 percent showed they expected it (b); 50 percent gave special treats (a); but only 12 percent included "do nothing at all" (c) among their choices. Most of the mothers seemed to know that if you focus on a child's inadequacies you can discourage him: Only 12 percent recalled showing their children "how it could be done better" (d).

  In Question 8, on handling misbehavior, 75 percent emphasized not punishment, but supplying feedback on a child's progress through discussion of expectations with him. Disappointment was indicated, but rarely anger or retribution. Scores were: (a) and (c), 77 percent; (d) 53 percent; (e) 40 percent; (f) 19 percent. Only 4 percent showed no reaction at all!

- *Climate of the home (9)* Seventy-two percent of the mothers described their homes as either "somewhat" or "extremely" calm and harmonious. Other evidence showed they put extra effort into maintaining this climate during difficult times. The majority had also described themselves as content, and more than a third said they were "extremely content" during their child-rearing years.

- *Ethical standards and other values (10,11)* In answer to Question 10, "be a good person" was chosen by more mothers (80 percent) as very important than any other item. Being happy was next, and attaining high standards was close behind; being well-liked was at the bottom, far below the others.

  When it came to Question 11, more than 60 percent of the mothers stressed "education and learning," values which show up strongly in the backgrounds of most successful people. This was true for both parents. Below is a list of their responses. It's interesting to note again the high emphasis on getting along with others ("be a good person") and the low emphasis on money and success, as well as the close similarity between mother's and father's emphasis.

	Emphasized by survey mothers	Emphasized by their husbands
Education and learning	62%	62%
Musical ability	12%	12%
Athletic ability	11%	24%
Money and financial success	4%	11%
Getting along with others	38%	29%
Being religious	12%	11%
Family closeness	40%	16%
Interest in science	5%	7%
Interest in art	9%	4%
Interest in current events, politics	12%	18%
Other_____	4%	2%

Are you raising an achiever?

- *Reading and watching TV (12,13)* Books and reading were of central importance, underscoring the high stress on education and learning. Question 12 revealed that 96 percent of the mothers read to their children when they were very small and read to them often, and most continued until their children were at least seven or eight, many far beyond that age. Thirty-eight percent reported home libraries of more than 200 volumes; many reported active use of local libraries. Radio and TV, according to Question 13, was not a major intrusion on family life, with 66 percent of the parents reporting their child spent less than five hours a week listening to the radio or watching television. (Your situation will probably be quite different.)

- *Children's enrichment (14,15)* Most of the parents—even those with limited incomes—managed to provide some additional instruction for their youngster outside school. Nearly 100 percent of the successful offspring got some sort of supplementary lessons, with music, sports, religion, and dance heading the list. Three-fourths of the families entertained at least several times a month, according to Question 15, and over a third entertained more than once a week. The inclusion of the children in these social events, bringing them into contact and providing discussion with all kinds of people, was cited by many mothers as a major source of stimulation and inspiration. It was also another indication of family closeness.

- *Mother's enrichment (16)* Our respondents kept up a number of personal activities and involvements of their own: working, taking classes, doing volunteer work, studying music, painting, writing. By maintaining a variety of pursuits, they were able to be concerned and interested parents as well as giving their children a model for independence.

   In seeing how your responses compare, remember that times have changed—the TV issue, for instance. But other things haven't, such as praise, affection, importance of reading and stimulation. Reviewing yourself and how your family lives may give you an opportunity to change a few things around and make life—and creating an achieving environment—a little easier for you and your family.

12. The twelve signposts for success

When we started this project we knew that no questionnaire or study could possibly encompass the many and changing ways in which parents bring up their children. Thousands of books have been written on every aspect of it, from toilet training to stepparenting, and still none of them, nor even all of them together, is quite the same as living the experience.

The object of our study was simple and very contemporary. We're living in an age where, thanks to the media, achievement is celebrated as never before. Magazines on subjects ranging from photography to stockbrokerage, television shows that cover cooking to comedy, are all bringing new faces before an interested and competitive audience. As a result, achievement is seen not only as desirable, but as possible for nearly everyone. One reads about the new star of a TV show, or the author of a million-copy-seller first novel, and finds that they're really not much different from oneself. They often have ordinary home lives, unimpressive backgrounds, everyday appearances. The myths of being born in a stage trunk, or enduring single-minded privation for years before attaining success, are over. It looks easy. There must be some simple secret, we say, something even I could do to succeed at what I want to do, or help my children succeed.

That feeling was the inspiration for this book. Knowing that we couldn't really find rules for creating a movie star, corporate head, scientist, or statesman, we took the broad view that the common element in all success stories is someone who has identified and applied his gifts—whatever they may be—to the fullest. There is room now, thanks to the variety of vocations and avocations we're busily practicing, for achievement in virtually any sphere, and a gratifying spirit of acknowledgment of it.

To learn how to foster achievement and motivation in growing children we applied to outstanding examples to find out how they had, literally, helped their children achieve achievement; and in doing so, achieved themselves. Their field, for our purposes, was mothering, and the acknowledgment of successful mothering is the raising of successful children. In this they succeeded admirably, so they are the stars of this show.

In putting together the anecdotes, survey data, advice, research studies, and other material in this book, we saw—as you may have—that again and again the same attitudes toward child-rearing emerged; the same approaches were shown, whether the subject was discipline, education, communications, or handling challenges of infancy or adolescence. Dr. Chance, in preparing the *Family Circle* article, identified these approaches as being so common in the backgrounds of achievers that he called them "signposts on the road to success." Our further research confirmed them and yielded a few more.

Probably the most illuminating new material came from achievers themselves. We wanted to see how they felt about child rearing, first because, as one survey mother had cautioned, "these answers are subjective, and my child might answer them quite differently." Second, because many of our achievers are now parents themselves, and we felt we could benefit from their two-way input. We asked a group of them, including survey children and others, what they would recommend to parents seeking to raise achievers now. Though they didn't know it, to our delight and gratification, they resoundingly affirmed the old-fashioned techniques that had worked so well for Mom.

Here then are twelve signposts, or basic approaches to successful child rearing that any parent can follow.

Signposts for Success

● 1. Recognize that *you* make a difference, both in what you do—the child-rearing choices you make, and in who you are—how you act as an example to your children.

Acknowledging your own impact on your child's future is probably the most fundamental acceptance of your role as a parent. As Dr. Chance put it, "How you rear your children will help shape their personalities and futures. If you insist on believing that success is in the hands of Fate, you are playing roulette with your child's future. The earlier you realize your influence as a positive force, the better." The survey mothers undeniably felt this. They shared a deep commitment to their children, a profound understanding of their roles in their children's lives.

The message is clear. Don't underestimate your importance in the child-rearing process. This covers not only training techniques, but less obvious matters like staying in good health and avoiding depression, a common affliction of self-sacrificing mothers who don't realize what a lasting and devastating effect it can have on their children. (Seek help if you need it—you're certainly entitled to it.)

It also means being aware that even the smallest things, incidents, conversations carry the hidden weight of the future. Rosalyn Yalow, mother and achiever, placed high value on parents as models: "The most important thing in raising children is how you behave. They see what you are and then they decide whether they like that or not. When you live with children, you can't fool them too long." One's example is far more important than the finer points of how one trains a child. Over and over again, our data proved this point. To raise achieving and motivated children, it is not so much the details of any particular life-style that matter. Instead, *it is the effect on your children of the way you live and behave.*

- 2. Don't be afraid to have high expectations for your children. Your faith in and hope for their futures will be their inspiration.

This was the first component of gifted mothering and a major theme in the survey data. The mothers believed in their children and worked to seek positive opportunities for them. In their turn, the children responded by striving to live up to their parents' expectations and merit the respect and faith they received. There's nothing quite so powerful as having someone on your side saying, "You can do it, kid," whatever it is you want to do. This belief in the child transcends any particular skills he may have or want at the moment; it's rather a belief in his right to capabilities and achievement. Many achievers remembered parental expectations of success, coupled with the belief they could do or be anything they wanted, as the greatest inducement to their early achievement.

- 3. Get close to your children, and stay close. Establish solid trust in the child as early as possible, to give him security and confidence.

We learned that children should have a very warm and affectionate relationship with at least one parent in order to establish that lifelong feeling of trust and self-confidence which is enormously helpful, if not actually a requirement, in achieving satisfying adulthood. This is Erik Erikson's first stage in the growth process.

Most parents do show a lot of attention and love to infants and young children, but *keeping* the relationship close and warm is just as important. It was a common factor in survey families, with communications cited as the main avenue of closeness with older children. An achiever advised, "Keep the lines of communication open, a pattern which can be established early, and take the time to *know* the children." Another said, "Where you watch, watch unobtrusively, but know what's going on. It's an essential support to a child."

This is especially true of the passage through adolescence. One mother said of her son, now a corporate leader, "We could always communicate. He liked to garden and to help me, and we would have long talks about all sorts of things....Relationships with children are extremely important. Some families make no effort to keep up with the children." An achiever said, "A good babysitter can stay with little kids, but with older children, life is unpredictable. You have to be more available emotionally."

Each parent has to experiment with ways to stay close to his growing child. It could be sharing hobbies, talking things over, or taking long walks—but it always means taking time to show that you care. It may mean time away from something you want to do, but as one achiever said, rather tartly, "Take the time to be committed. Share with them, respect them; otherwise, don't have them."

Of course the most profound expression of parental closeness is simply loving the children in such a way that they are aware of it and secure in it. This is the basis of *all* successful child rearing, because when love is in place, closeness and all other signposts can be set much more easily. Ehrma Filer's one-sentence wisdom says it all; when we asked her for the one piece of advice she'd give mothers raising children today, she said, "Just love 'em a lot and let 'em know it!"

- 4. Don't be too controlling. Give your children the freedom to learn and do things on their own. It helps build self-reliance.

This might also be called "granting autonomy in a supportive environment." Once again, the seeds can be sown in early childhood. Letting children discover things and make judgments on their own, even at very early ages, gives them the decision-making experience they need to stand on their own later. Dr. Chance, referring to this as "providing room for growth" said, "Many parents of low achievers impose so many rules and exert so much control that the child's judgment and initiative never develop. When the soup boils over, a parent often complains, 'The house could burn to the ground and you wouldn't even bother to call the fire department.' But before you berate a child, ask yourself, 'Have I given the youngster enough opportunities for responsibility?'"

As we know, self-reliance was seen as a key to motivation and achievement, both among the survey children and in many other studies of achievers. This doesn't mean you should leave children completely on their own or in sole charge; it means let them make mistakes in a safe environment, knowing your love will still be there even when they trip and fall. As one achiever said, "Help them with the decision-making process, whenever they are ready for it, so they'll be doing things on their own, but with your complete backing." And another: "Emphasize self-reliance: in decision making, in responsibility for their own lives and actions." And a third: "Teach them to be highly flexible and adaptable, so they can respond to the world about them.... Constantly emphasize that the career they are thinking of at the moment may not be the one that works out; give them a wide range of experiences...."

You may remember that in the chapter on self-reliance, many achievers claimed that having the freedom to follow their own stars was also a major factor in getting them started on the road to achievement, as was parental closeness and support.

- 5. Make your home as stable and harmonious as possible.

This is self-explanatory. Over 80 percent of the survey homes had both parents on hand for the child-rearing years, so there's a correlation between this kind of stability and achievement. But in the present age, it seems that the stability created by having a reliable centeredness to the home, whether there are one or two working or nonworking parents on hand is really the important thing.

When it comes to harmony, the majority of the survey mothers described their home lives as harmonious and themselves as content, many of them saying they were extremely harmonious and content. If you and your spouse argue much of the time, and there's a general tone of tension and bickering in the household, it's probably not a pleasant place to be. Children will stay away, either holed up in their rooms, or at friends' houses, or wherever else they can escape—sometimes to places you wouldn't be too pleased about. And if they stay away, or aren't much fun when they are around, neither you nor they are going to get the great benefit of positive family life which seemed to prevail in most survey homes.

Dr. Chance suggested this solution: "One thing you can do immediately is try to change your *own* behavior: become aware of your *own* tendency to shout, to criticize unnecessarily, to bicker. Try to spend more time listening to your child; make an effort to do more things together. You may be surprised by how a few simple changes in your behavior will improve the home situation dramatically. That, in turn, should produce some very favorable changes in your child."

If you feel you could use professional help, contact your local mental health association, clinic, or social agency and ask for appropriate public agencies and therapists in private practice. There will be a number of qualified people to select from, with a range of fees. Feel free to ask for complete information and alternative choices. Never be shy about making any kind of positive change. It can mean much more to your children than you realize, and you may feel able to do it for them even if you're uncertain of making changes for yourself—and you certainly deserve it as much as they do.

- 6. Provide stimulation and challenges from outside. Make your home a learning place.

This was a component of the gifted mother's intense involvement in the early stages; as the children got older the providing of outside stimulation translated into a heavy involvement in the outside world, especially the world of learning. When children are very young, the stimulation takes the form of cuddling and loving, singing, talking, and playing with them. The more time spent in such pursuits, the more rapidly the child's intellectual faculties develop. This role even has a name: You're a mediator of the environment when you do this with your youngster.

After the children reach school age, the technique is the same: Spend time helping interpret the world to your child, but recognize that you have a partner in the schools. Just as in all the other signposts, intention is all-important. As Dr. Chance remarked, "Routinely asking a child, 'What did you learn in school today?' insufficiently stresses the importance of education." Taking children places, providing outside lessons, encouraging them in hobbies, helping them with reading and homework, bringing home things from your work and activities to share, are all part of this.

The most important thing about this signpost is that most parents are unaware of it. They're standing on a gold mine of opportunity to enrich their children's lives without ever using it. For one thing, the greatest armor you can bring to the war against TV in your child's life is to offer yourself as a stimulating companion-teacher instead. You not only help your child enormously in advancing his understanding and feeling for knowledge as an exciting adventure, you get to share time and enthusiasm with him.

- 7. Encourage your children's gifts and talents; the earlier the better.

We felt this was directly connected to the mothers' intense involvement with, and high expectations for, their children. In spending many hours in stimulating play and contact with the child, while watching his reactions closely, they may have been able to spot early gifts and abilities that a less-involved parent might have overlooked.

Not only did they identify such gifts, they often inspired them by taking the children to concerts, the ballet, science fairs, zoos, and so on. Sometimes they taught them how to sing or play musical instruments, or to paint or sew. There's a name for this, too: It's called the culture bearer. This passing along of the aesthetic or nonpractical aspects of culture is one of the ancient and often enjoyable rights—and rites—of parenthood.

Once the child did respond, parents responded in turn, by the "hot coal technique" of providing encouragement, lessons, materials, books, or even taking trips to places where the child's interest led. Sustaining this kind of support over long periods, and helping the child to the difficult place where his own motivation to continue must take over, is one of the great challenges of raising achievers, particularly in creative fields. A distinguishing feature of parents who performed this delicate balancing act successfully was that they were able to let go when the child's interest waned, or support a new interest with as much enthusiasm. Helping the child attain the fullest expression of his gifts was the mark of this signpost.

- 8. Set reasonable standards of performance and expect them to be met. This is another key to self-reliance.

Of course loving a child and granting autonomy doesn't mean indulging him. Said Dr. Chance, "The well-adjusted child meets standards, lives up to his potential, doesn't just 'get by.' This applies to social behavior as well as to school or work achievements. If a parent condones a half-baked effort, there's no incentive to do one's best."

There is no doubt that the survey mothers expected their children to strive for—and attain—excellence. The earliest expressions of this were their demands for accomplishment in simple tasks like picking up their rooms and doing homework at early ages. Later, when it came to schoolwork, Michael Crichton's mother answered a query about the importance of not failing in school by saying "The failure would have been not to *try*."

Having standards is actually, according to the experts, much more reassuring to children than being without them. Children allowed to do utterly as they please often flounder, directionless, feeling their parents don't care rather than being grateful for the unbidden opportunity to "find themselves."

If you know your child is capable of better marks or more considerate or responsible behavior, ask for them. Asking for his best effort is a powerful way of saying you're aware of his capabilities and willing to demand them, even if his teachers or friends aren't. This also reinforces the self-reliance he'll need to keep achieving to the maximum of his ability—even if it means he must leave others behind. As one achiever said, "Self-reliance helps an individual feel free of the pressures toward conformity, to avoid the crowd, and set his own sights."

- 9. Accentuate the positive: Give praise over blame. It builds self-esteem.

Parents often get into the habit of ignoring children's successes and only turning the full blare of their attention to them when they misbehave or disappoint. Dr. Chance felt "It is probably essential that children learn early that success is worth striving for, that their efforts are appreciated, that their accomplishments are noticed." It's easy to reward a small child to reinforce his desirable behavior. You can hug and kiss him, praise him, give him a cookie, display his artwork and school papers, tell relatives and friends how proud you are of him.

Older children need this recognition too, but you may have to think a little harder before finding ways to express it. Start by asking yourself, "What is my child doing well? Have I shown him that I'm aware of it? Do other family members, or neighbors, or teachers give him respect and approval?" You can then offer positive feedback, as well as suitable rewards, such as a day off from chores, or a mini-shopping spree for something he or she really wants. Often parents have many things to be grateful for in their children that aren't too visible, such as kindness to older relatives, care in appearance or room tidiness, or faithful piano practice. Learn to be aware of these accomplishments and say so.

Many survey parents spoke of being "fortunate in having such good children," and they seemed well aware of—and vocal about—their children's positive behavior. They disciplined them in the same way: by withholding privileges, offering negative feedback, and letting them know they expected better. This, rather than punishment, which diminishes feelings of worth, seemed to be the object of discipline. As one achiever put it, "Accept failures—never dwell on them— as stepping-stones. Give children a strong sense of inner self-confidence and self-worth."

- 10. Establish high ideals and a healthy respect for the rights of others.

This was an interesting finding of the survey: The parents put great emphasis on establishing high ethical standards among their children. They felt it gave them something to "lean on" as well as to gain benefit from in their own lives. They taught, and exemplified, upstanding behavior toward relatives, friends, and the community, as well as being courteous within the family circle. Money was not a consideration in this: Well-to-do children didn't condescend to those less better off; those with less didn't seem to resent those with more.

We know that the mothers rated "be a good person" as among the highest virtues, far above being well liked. While these mothers certainly expected their children to achieve excellence, it was clear they wanted them to get along with others and be decent, honest people—in other words, to succeed, but fairly—not by stepping on others.

This is a far cry from the "nice guys finish last" ethic one is often told to expect from highly competitive, successful people. It seemed to run strongly through the survey sample, and was yet another way in which parents taught their children to be self-reliant. By learning, as children, to follow their own moral code, which might be much higher and stricter than the one prevailing in "the gang," they can acquire the self-assurance to do what they think is right in the teeth of much tougher resistance when they get older.

This can also be a challenge for parents. As children hit the tricky ground of adolescence, their role as examples comes strongly to the foreground. The children's questions about sexual behavior, religious beliefs, moral values, and political preferences take time to answer, and can't be answered at all unless parents know where *they* stand. Asking your children to uphold standards of social behavior—such as not doing things other children are doing—is one thing, and may be quite appropriate. Asking them not to do what *you* are doing is quite another. Facing this challenge squarely can lead to a renewal of standards for parents as well as being a learning experience for your maturing children.

• 11. Remember, it's the quality, not the quantity, of the time you spend with your child that counts.

We've discussed this at length in the chapter on single-parent and working-mother households, but it's really important for every parent. When you're truly listening and looking at what they're telling and showing, your children know it and appreciate it. Just letting them pass by or be around you within the same four walls isn't the same as giving them specific time and attention, however limited it may be. One of the most common misunderstandings of parents is that once the activities children shared with them are replaced by those the children have on their own, parents no longer play an active role. Actually, many a teenager with a schedule even more demanding than mother's or dad's still has a head full of questions and confusion. He needs your time and attention as much as, if not more than, he did when you had to tie his shoelaces.

Make those hours count, no matter how few they are. And if they're many, make a few really count. They are the stuff memories—and achiever's inspirations—are made of.

- 12. Think of yourself. Put some real time and attention into developing yourself as an individual.

This may seem like a tall order after all our advice about giving time and attention to your children, but it's every bit as important, especially if you're a stay-at-home mom. As the article reported, "It is traditional to praise mothers by saying how devoted they are to their children ('Her children come first'; 'She'd do anything for her kids'). But the mothers of our notables weren't martyrs, sacrificing their lives to their children. While they definitely showed intense interest in their children, they invested time and energy in a number of activities outside the home."

We know they did everything from studying foreign languages to running for political office to teaching Sunday school. The evidence was that far from injuring the child, such outside activity probably inspired him to do things on his own, just as mother did. Mother's working on self-improvement, meshing it into her busy schedule, and interest in a variety of different activities, would all provide a superb model for any youngster to imitate. In addition, it doubtless kept her from feeling the frustration suffered by many women who give all their time and talents to their young children; these talents then fall into disuse as the children become older and more independent. You can preserve yourself, and your family, by growing into outside involvements as they do.

Father also played an active role by supporting mother's interest in adding to her outside life, and often by having a few special interests of his own. Many of the fathers were sports fans, and a good number were also involved in hobbies, music, crafts, and other pastimes. There are dozens of ways in which two active partners, or those in single-parent homes, can bring their energies to bear in creating interesting lives for themselves and compelling examples for their children.

Certainly following these twelve signposts won't guarantee fame and fortune for your child. Rearing a child is not a simple matter; each child is different—endowments and personalities vary, and the circumstances of upbringing are constantly changing. Bearing in mind that no one can provide a recipe for creating a genius, or a geologist, or a geographer, for that matter, we think the experiences we've described in this book are so prevalent in the backgrounds of high achievers that they must have played an important role in the achievers' success. Since they are experiences any parent can provide, we hope they can be useful and inspiring guidelines to parents who are interested in helping their children reach their potential—which is what we think makes an achiever.

Appendix 1: the survey questionnaire

Name: _____ Address: _____

1. What is your place of birth: _____
                                             City   State   Country

2. What is your husband's* place of birth: _____
                                                           City State Country

3. What is your race (check one): Black _____
White _____ Hispanic _____ Other _____

*Please note: Throughout this questionnaire, in using "husband" we are referring to the child's father, or male parent who helped you raise the child.

4. When you were growing up, did you spend most of your childhood in (check one): Farm _____ Town (up to 100,000 pop.) _____ City (over 100,000) _____ Suburb _____

5. What is your religion? What is your husband's religious preference? (Check one in each column):

	Your own	Husband's
Catholic	( )	( )
Protestant	( )	( )
Jewish	( )	( )
None	( )	( )
Other:_____	( )	( )

6. Would you say you are (check one): Very religious _____ Somewhat religious _____ Not at all religious _____

7. What is your political preference (check one): Very Liberal _____ Somewhat Liberal _____ Moderate _____ Somewhat Conservative _____ Conservative _____

8. As your child was growing up (until 18 years old), were you separated, divorced, or widowed? Yes _____ No _____ If yes, how old was your child when this occurred? _____ If this occurred again, how old was the child the second time? _____

9. When your child was young (under 12), was your husband away from home for an extended period? Yes _____ No _____ If yes, for how long (check one): About 6 months _____ One year _____ Two years _____ Three or more years _____

10. Were you employed at any point while your child was living at home? Yes _____ No _____ If yes: How old was your child when you began to work? _____ About how many hours a week did you work? Less than 20 _____ 20–40 _____ Over 40 hours _____ Did you work continuously for more than 2 years? Yes _____ No _____ If yes, how many years in all did you work? _____ What was the nature of your work? _____

11. What level of education did you complete? What level of education did your husband complete? (Check one in each column):

The survey questionnaire

	Your own	Husband's
No formal education	( )	( )
Grade school	( )	( )
High school	( )	( )
Some college	( )	( )
College graduate	( )	( )
Highest advanced degree:	_____	_____

12. What was your husband's occupation while your child was growing up? _____

13. When your child was under 18 years old, what was your combined family income (check one): Under $5,000 _____ $5,000–10,000 _____ $10,000–15,000 _____ $15,000–20,000 _____ Over $20,000 _____

14. During this period, would you say your family's economic situation generally (check one): Improved rapidly _____ Improved slowly _____ Stayed the same _____ Worsened slowly _____ Worsened rapidly _____

15. Listed below are various activities and areas of interest. Which appealed to you and your husband while your child was living at home? (Check columns for all such activities):

	Of interest to:	
	You	Your husband
a. Music, literature, painting, other artistic areas	( )	( )
b. Science (Read science magazines, visited museums, used a telescope, microscope, etc.)	( )	( )
c. Business (Concerned with job, career or office; making money, investments etc.)	( )	( )
d. Family (Spent time with spouse and children; concerned with children's activities in school, etc.)	( )	( )
e. Sports and outdoor activities (As participant or fan)	( )	( )

	Of interest to:	
	You	Your husband
f. Social (Enjoyed being with friends for conversation, cards, to pass time of day; belonged to lodges, clubs)	( )	( )
g. Workshop and crafts (Enjoyed making things around house)	( )	( )
h. Politics (Took part in local or national politics; was an avid reader of current political events)	( )	( )
i. Furthering education (Getting diploma or degree, other professional advancement)	( )	( )
j. Other: _____	( )	( )

16. Which of these interests was *most* important to you? _____ Next most important to you? _____ Most important to your husband? _____

17. As you think about the time when your child was at home, would you say you were usually (check one): Extremely content _____ Content _____ Discontent _____ Extremely discontent _____

18. Please list the birthdates of *all* your children in order. Place a check (✓) next to your famous son or daughter.

	Date of Birth (mo./day/year)	Sex	(✓)	Present occupation	If deceased, age at death
1.					
2.					
3.					
4.					
5.					
6.					

19. Which child was generally your favorite? _____ (use number above). Which child was generally your husband's favorite? _____

20. Of these choices, check the *two* you like most about small children (under 12):

The survey questionnaire

When they are neat and clean ( )
When they hug and kiss you ( )
Playing with them ( )
When they do what you tell them to ( )
When they're well-mannered with others ( )
When they finally learn to do something after a long time ( )
When they play nicely with other children ( )

21. In which of the following did your child spend most of his or her childhood? (check one): Farm _____ Town (up to 100,000 pop.) _____ City (over 100,000) _____ Suburb _____

22. Please circle the approximate age that your child began these activities:
Crawl:
3 mos.   6 mos.   9 mos.   12 mos.   18 mos. or older
Walk:
6 mos.   9 mos.   12 mos.   18 mos.   2 yrs. or older
Speak (in complete sentences):
12 mos.   18 mos.   2 yrs.   3 yrs.   4 yrs. or older
Read:
18 mos.   2 yrs.   3 yrs.   4 yrs.   5 yrs. or older

23. When your child was an infant, did you feed him or her on a (check one): demand schedule (whenever the baby cried) _____ fixed schedule (every 4 hours or so) _____

24. Was your child frequently cared for by others? Please check all appropriate spaces: Grandparent(s) _____ Older brother or sister _____ Other relatives _____ Babysitter _____ Housekeeper/Nursemaid _____ Other:_____

25. Did your child attend (check and fill in appropriate spaces):
Nursery school ( )
Public school   ( )   Total number of years _____
Private school ( )   Total number of years _____

26. When your child was attending school, did he have any of the following common problems? Check all appropriate spaces: Difficulties with teacher _____ Difficulties with classmates _____ Learning problems _____ Dislike the school _____ Disciplinary problems _____

27. In general, who was primarily responsible for the discipline of your children (check one): You _____ Your husband _____ Other _____

28. How would you rate the discipline your child received during childhood (check one): Very strict _____ Strict _____ Lenient _____ Very lenient _____

29. In general, who did your child feel closer to (check one): You _____ Your husband _____ Equally to both _____

30. Would you say that your child is (check one): More similar to you than your husband _____ More similar to your husband than to you _____ Not similar to either parent _____

31. As your child was growing up (until age 18), would you say that your family life was generally (check one):
Extremely turbulent and emotional ( )
Somewhat turbulent and emotional ( )
Somewhat calm and harmonious ( )
Extremely calm and harmonious ( )

32. When your child was young (under 12), and fulfilled your expectations, or was "good," how did you react? (Check *three* of these items.)
Gave him a special treat or privilege ( )
Showed him you expected it ( )
Kissed or hugged him to show how pleased you were ( )
Showed him how it could have been done even better ( )
Did nothing at all to make it seem special ( )
Told him what a good boy he was. Praised him for being good. ( )

33. When your child was young (under 12), and misbehaved or disappointed you, how did you react? (Check *three* of these items.)

Showed him you were disappointed in him.	( )
Didn't show any feeling about it.	( )
Pointed out how he should have behaved.	( )
Scolded or spanked him.	( )
Deprived him of something he liked or wanted.	( )
Just waited until he did what you wanted.	( )

34. At approximately what age did you expect your child to do the following things. Please circle the appropriate age.
To know his way around the neighborhood.
4 years   5 yrs.   6 yrs.   7 yrs.   8 yrs.   9 or older
To hang up his own clothes and look after his own possessions.
4 yrs.   5 yrs.   6 yrs.   7 yrs.   8 yrs.   9 or older
To take part in his parents' interests.
4 yrs.   5 yrs.   6 yrs.   7 yrs.   8 yrs.   9 or older
To do homework by himself.
4 yrs.   5 yrs.   6 yrs.   7 yrs.   8 yrs.   9 or older
To buy something at the store alone.
4 yrs.   5 yrs.   6 yrs.   7 yrs.   8 yrs.   9 or older

35. When your child was growing up, how important did you think it was that he grow up to (check one for each item):

	Very	Some-what	Not very	Not at all
a. be a good person	( )	( )	( )	( )
b. be independent	( )	( )	( )	( )
c. be happy	( )	( )	( )	( )
d. attain a standard of excellence or high achievement	( )	( )	( )	( )
e. be well-liked	( )	( )	( )	( )

36. Which one of the above did you consider *most* important?
_____ (use letter above)

37. When your child was young (under 12), how much emphasis did you place on (check one for each item):

	Great deal	Some	Very little	None at all
a. protecting him, worrying about his welfare	( )	( )	( )	( )
b. providing strict discipline	( )	( )	( )	( )
c. your being involved in his daily activities	( )	( )	( )	( )

38. Mothers often set limits on their children's behavior. Place a check next to those restrictions you remember having placed on your child:

Not to be noisy and boisterous in the house.	( )
To be respectful and not interfere with adults.	( )
Not to be sloppy at the table or eat with his fingers.	( )
Not to play with children he doesn't know or of whom his parents don't approve	( )
Not to fail at schoolwork.	( )
Not to depend on his mother for suggestions for what to do with his time.	( )
Not to spend money without consulting his parents.	( )

39. Of the following attributes or talents, which three did you most emphasize to your growing child? Which three do you think your husband tried to emphasize? (Check *three* in each column.)

	Emphasized by:	
	You	Your husband
Education and learning	( )	( )
Musical ability	( )	( )
Athletic ability	( )	( )
Money and financial success	( )	( )
Getting along with others	( )	( )
Being religious	( )	( )
Family closeness	( )	( )
Interest in science	( )	( )
Interest in art	( )	( )
Interest in current events, politics	( )	( )
Other_____	( )	( )

The survey questionnaire

40. Did your child usually receive an allowance. (A specific amount of money each week)? Yes _____ No _____ If yes, at what age did he first receive this allowance? _____ How did you encourage your child to handle his own money (check one):

To pay his own expenses (lunch, carfare, etc.)	( )
To spend on luxuries, recreation, etc.	( )
To save it at home or in the bank	( )

41. Most children have some problems while they are growing up (until 18 years old). Which of the following areas was a special problem for your child? (Check as many as apply.)

Poor eyesight	( )
Poor hearing	( )
Overweight/Underweight	( )
Too short/Too tall	( )
Eating	( )
Toilet training	( )
Bed wetting	( )
Thumb sucking	( )
Nail biting	( )
Nightmares	( )
Specific fears (of dark, heights, etc.)	( )
Unspecified worries	( )
Allergies (asthma, food, etc.)	( )
Serious illness (polio, tuberculosis, etc.)	( )
Reading difficulties	( )
Speech difficulties	( )
Being a "difficult" child	( )
Other: _____	( )

42. When your child was young (under 12) was any member of your immediate family seriously ill (physically or mentally), handicapped (paralysis, blindness, etc.) or alcoholic? Yes _____ No _____ If yes, check as many family members as necessary:

Mother	( )
Father	( )
Brother	( )
Sister	( )
Grandparent	( )

43. Was your child particularly close to any of his brothers or sisters? Yes _____ No _____ If yes, which?

Older brother	( )
Older sister	( )
Younger brother	( )
Younger sister	( )

44. Would you say that when your child was living at home he or she generally (check one):

Had many friends	( )
Had few friends	( )
Had one close friend	( )
Was basically a "loner"	( )

45. Did you ever read books to your child? Yes _____ No _____ If yes, about how old was he when you began to read to him and when you stopped reading to him? _____ years old to _____ years old. About how many times a week did you usually read to your child? (check one):

Every day	( )
A few times a week	( )
At least once a week	( )
Two or three times a month	( )

46. When your child was growing up, about how many books were available to him in your home (check one):

Under 50	( )
Between 50 and 200	( )
Between 200 and 500	( )
Over 500	( )

47. When your child was young (under 12 years old), did he often listen to the radio or watch television? Yes _____ No _____ If yes, about how many hours a week? (check one):

Less than 5 hours	( )
Between 5 and 10 hours	( )
Between 10 and 20 hours	( )
Over 20 hours	( )

48. When you and your husband went on vacation, did you generally (check one): Take the children (   ) Leave the children home (   ) Rarely took vacations (   )

49. When your child was living at home, how often did you entertain friends or family (check one):
More than once a week   (   )
A few times a month   (   )
Once a month   (   )
Once every other month   (   )
Once or twice a year   (   )

50. As a youngster, did your child ever take special lessons outside school? Yes _____ No _____ If yes, please check as many activities as apply:
Tap, modern dance, or ballet lessons   (   )
Music lessons   (   )
    Instruments(s): _____
Sports instruction   (   )
    Specify: _____
Riding lessons   (   )
Acting lessons   (   )
Foreign language instruction   (   )
Religious training   (   )
Private tutor   (   )
    Subject(s): _____
Other: _____   (   )

51. When your child was young (under 12), did he ever do or have the following (check appropriate spaces):
Imaginary playmates   (   )
Collections (stamps, coins, etc.)   (   )
    Specify: _____
Special hobby   (   )
    Specify: _____

52. At what age did your child leave home to live on his or her own? _____ years

53. What would you say was *your* most important contribution, as a mother, to the success of your child?

54. Can you think of any particular event or influence that may have contributed to your child's success? Please describe briefly.

55. What would you say was the major problem you encountered in raising your son or daughter?

56. If you could raise your child again, is there anything you would do differently?

Appendix 2: sources

References for the research cited in this book are given below in the order the citations appear in the chapters.

1. The study to find out what worked

Dorothy Lewis, J. H. Pincus, S. S. Shanok, and G. H. Glaser, "Violent Juvenile Delinquents: Psychiatric, Neurological, Psychological and Abuse Factors," *Journal of the American Academy of Child Psychiatry* 18 (1978), pp. 307-319.

John Gardner, *Self-Renewal, the Individual and the Innovative Society* (New York: Harper & Row, 1963), p. 18.

Margaret W. Matlin and David J. Stang, *The Pollyanna Principle* (Cambridge: Schenkman, 1979).

2. The earth for the roots: the achievers' backgrounds

Charles G. Burck, "A Group Profile of the Fortune 500 Chief Executives," *Fortune*, May 1976.

George Davis, "A Healing Hand in Harlem," *The New York Times Magazine*, April 22, 1979.
Statistical Abstracts of the United States, U. S. Department of Commerce, Bureau of the Census, 1950.
David D. McClelland, *The Achieving Society* (New York: The Free Press, 1961).
Charles P. Smith, "The Origin and Expression of Achievement-Related Motives in Childhood" in Charles P. Smith, ed., *Achievement-Related Motives in Children* (New York: Russell Sage Foundation, 1969).
Kenneth Keniston, *All Our Children* (New York: Harcourt, Brace Jovanovich, 1977).
Kenneth Keniston, quoted in "The Future of the American Family," *Parents' Magazine*, August 1978.
Robert B. Zajonc, "Family Configuration and Intelligence Variations in Scholastic Aptitude Scores Parallel Trends in Family Size and the Spacing of Children," *Science*, April 1976.
Richard D. Lyons' review of "What Research Shows About Birth Order, Personality, and I.Q.," National Institute of Mental Health (1979) *The New York Times*, February 6, 1979.
Nan Robertson, "A Shy Designer Who Shocks, But Only With His Designs," *The New York Times*, July 29, 1976.
John Skow, "The Man Behind the Frog," *Time*, December 25, 1978.
William Stockton, "Celebrating Einstein," *The New York Times*, February 18, 1979.
Nan Robertson, "Barbara Tuchman, A Loner at the Top of Her Field," *The New York Times*, February 27, 1979.
Daniel Goleman, "1,528 Little Geniuses and How They Grew," *Psychology Today*, February 1980.

3. Gifted mothering: the threefold commitment

Garwood S. Gray, "First Name Stereotypes as a Factor in Self-Concept and School Achievement," *Journal of Education Psychology*, 68(4) (1976), p. 482.
H. Harari and J. W. McDavid, "Name Stereotypes and Teacher Expectations," *Journal of Educational Psychology* 65 (1974) p. 222.

J. W. McDavid and H. Harari, "Stereotyping of Names and Popularity in Grade School Children," *Child Development* 37 (1966), p. 453.

Robert Sears, Eleanor Maccoby, and Harry Levin, *Patterns of Child Rearing* (New York: Harper & Row, 1957) p. 28.

Robert Rosenthal and Lenore Jacobson, *Pygmalion in the Classroom* (New York: Holt, Rinehart & Winston, 1968).

Robert Rosenthal, "The Pygmalion Effect Lives," *Psychology Today* (September 1973).

Earl Schaefer and Nancy Bayley, "Maternal Behavior, Child Behavior and their Inter-Correlations from Infancy through Adolescence," *Monographs of the Society for Research in Child Development* 28 (1963), p. 3.

Earl Schaefer and Nancy Bayley, "Correlations of Maternal and Child Behaviors with the Development of Mental Abilities," *Monographs of the Society for Research in Child Development* 24 (1964), p. 6.

Elizabeth Bing, "Effect of Child-Rearing Practices on Development of Differential Cognitive Abilities," *Child Development* 34 (1963), pp. 631-648.

Amy Gross, "Dunaway—the Woman," *Vogue*, March 1979.

George Davis, *A Healing Hand in Harlem*.

Erik Erikson, *Childhood and Society* (New York: W. W. Norton, 1950), p. 249.

Margaret Mahler, *The Psychological Birth of the Human Infant* (New York: Basic Books, 1967).

Louise J. Kaplan, *Oneness and Separateness, from Infant to Individual* (New York: Simon and Schuster, 1978).

David McClelland, *The Achieving Society*.

K. Allison Clarke-Stewart, "Interactions Between Mothers and Their Young Children," *Monographs of the Society for Research in Child Development* 38 (1973), pp. 6-7.

Aaron Stern, *The Making of a Genius* (Miami: Hurricane House, 1971).

Richard Haitch, "Prodigy," *The New York Times*, February 27, 1977.

Rene Spitz, M.D., "Hospitalism: An inquiry in the Genesis of Psychiatric Conditions in Early Childhood," *Psychoanalytic Study of the Child, Vol. 1* (New York: International Universities Press, 1945).

4. Gifted mothering and the hot coal technique

Natalie Gittelson, " 'Mom Sills' and 'Bubbly'—Two Lives in Tune," *The New York Times Magazine*, May 13, 1979.
Interview with Phyllis Cohen, PhD, Research Associate, Child Study Center, Yale School of Medicine, May 1979.
Gittelson, *op. cit.*
Howard Gardner, "Exploring the Mystery of Creativity," *The New York Times*, March 28, 1979.
John Gilmore, *The Productive Personality* (San Francisco: Albion Publishing, 1974).

5. Mothers and fathers: sharing the commitment and the parenting partnership

Ross D. Parke, "The Father of the Child," *The Sciences*, April 1979.
Ross D. Parke and Douglas B. Sawin, "Fathering: It's a Major Role," *Psychology Today*, November 1977.
James Atlas, "John Updike," *The New York Times Magazine*, December 10, 1978.
John Updike, *The Centaur* (New York: Alfred A. Knopf, 1963) p. 78.
Cheryl Bentsen, "The Brightest Kids," *New York* magazine, June 18, 1979.
Daniel Goleman, "1,528 Little Geniuses and How They Grew."
Melita Oden, "The Fulfillment of Promise: 40-year Follow-up of the Terman Gifted Group," *Genetic Psychological Monographs* 77, 1968, pp. 3-94.
James E. Anthony, "The Syndrome of the Psychologically Invulnerable Child," in *The Child in His Family; Children at Psychiatric Risk: Yearbook of the International Association for Child Psychiatry and Allied Professions*, Vol. 3, James E. Anthony, and Cyrille Koupernik, eds. (New York: John Wiley & Sons, 1974) pp. 429-544.
Ray Birdwhistell, "Personal Communication," quoted in James W. Ramey, *Intimate Friendships* (Englewood Cliffs: Prentice-Hall, 1976).

Cynthia Pincus, N. Radding, R. Lawrence, and R. Siegel, "Counseling Women in the Seventies: Response to a New Need," *Social Work*, March 1974.

Joann Vanek, "Time Spent in Housework," *Scientific American*, November 1974.

6. The family life that fosters achievement

Richard Meryman, "A Wyeth Comes Out of Hiding," *The New York Times Magazine*, January 7, 1979.

Frank Rich, "Warren Beatty," *Time*, July 3, 1978.

Glen H. Elder, "Parental Power Legitimation and Its Effect on the Adolescent," in *Readings in Adolescent Behavior and Development*, Hill and Shelton, eds. (Englewood Cliffs: Prentice-Hall, 1971).

Robert Coles, *Privileged Ones: The Well-Off and the Rich in America*, vol. 5, *Children of Crisis* (Boston: Little, Brown, 1977), p. 26

Sidney B. Simon, Leland W. Howe, and Howard Kirschenbaum, *Values Clarification* (New York: Hart Publishing Co., 1972).

7. Raising children for self-reliance: A key to achievement

James P. Comer, *Beyond Black and White* (New York: Quadrangle Books, 1972), p. 47.

Leslie Bennetts, "When the Parent Abdicates—Children Who Take On Adult Roles," *The New York Times*, March 6, 1978.

Robert Coles, *Privileged Ones*.

Barbara G. Harrison, "John Travolta—His Mother's Story," *McCall's*, July 1978.

Daniel Sugarman, Ph.D., *Priceless Gifts* (New York: Macmillan, 1978).

Sheila Feld, "Longitudinal Study of the Origins of Achievement Strivings," *Journal of Personality and Social Psychology*, 1967 (7), pp. 408-414.

George E. Vaillant, *Adaptation to Life* (Boston: Little, Brown, 1977).

8. Inspirations for achievement: role models, mentors, and the dream

Daniel J. Levinson with Charlotte Darrow, Edward Klein, Maria Levinson and Braxton McKee, *The Seasons of a Man's Life* (New York: Alfred A. Knopf, 1978).
James Coughey, "Media Mentors," *Psychology Today*, September, 1978.
Donna Summer interview on Rona Barrett Television Special, ABC, January 1, 1979.

9. Education is a full-time adventure

Mary Cable, *The Little Darlings* (New York: Scribners, 1977), p. 77.
Marcia Cohen, "How Do Prominent Parents Govern Their Children's TV Habits?" *The New York Times*, March 30, 1980.
Victor Goertzel and Mildred Goertzel, *Cradles of Eminence* (Boston: Little, Brown, 1962).
Richard Reeves, "How I Became a Supporter of and Appalled by Docudrama," *Panorama*, March 1980.
Ann Roe, "A Psychological Study of Eminent Psychologists and Anthropologists, and a Comparison with Biological and Physical Scientists," *Psychological Monographs* 67(2), 1953.
Ann Roe, "Crucial Life Experiences in the Development of Scientists" in *Talent and Education*, F. Torrance, ed., Minneapolis (University of Minnesota Press, 1960).
John H. Douglas, "The Genius of Everyman," *Science News*, April 23, 1977.

10. Bringing up achievers in single-parent and working-mother households

Statistical Abstracts of the United States, U. S. Department of Commerce, Bureau of the Census, 1978.
Melita Oden, "The Fulfillment of Promise."
Interview with Stephen L. Dworkin, MSW, Southern Connecticut State College, March 1979.

Index

A
Achievement
 role of family life in, 79-104
 role models in, 122-31
 importance of self-reliance, 105-14
Achievers
 backgrounds of, 14-29
 late bloomers, 29
 parental test, 160-66
 physical development of, 24-25
 in single parent and working mother households, 151-52
Adversity, uses of, 103-4
Atlas, James, 66

B
Bacharach, Bert, 65
Bacharach, Burt, 4, 65, 114
 mother, 58, 65, 130, 149
Barany, Kate, 39, 63, 71, 91, 158
Barany, Kenneth, 91
Barany, Sarah, 91
Barany family, 27, 85, 124
Barber, Samuel, 55
Barton, Clara, 133
Bayley, Nancy, 36
Beatty, Warren, 92
Bell, Larry, 4
Bergen, Candice, 124
Beyond Black and White (Comer), 109
Birdwhistell, Ray, 72
Bloom, Floyd, 4
 mother, 97
Buck, Pearl, 133

C
Cable, Mary, 132
Callahan, Daniel, 4, 35, 82, 110-11
Casals, Pablo, 133
Centaur, The (Updike), 66
Chance, Paul, 2, 172, 173, 176, 177, 178, 179, 180
Chase, Chevy, 3
Child abuse, 6
Child rearing experts, 7
Children of Crisis (Coles), 95
Chinn, Lulu, 38
Chinn, May, 16, 38
Clarke, John Clem, 4, 93
 mother, 93
Clarke-Stewart, Allison, 46
Cohen, Joel, 21, 90, 133
Cohen, Phyllis, 51, 53, 54, 57, 58
Coles, Robert, 95, 113
Comer, James, 109
Committee to Combat Huntingdon's Disease, 130
Crichton, Michael, 4, 11, 26, 52-53, 85, 97, 114
Crichton, Zula, 52-53, 63-64, 71, 84, 85, 87, 97, 180

D
Davis, George, 16
Discipline, importance of, 116-17
Douglas, Mike, 37
Dunaway, Faye, 3, 10, 52, 133
 mother, 37, 97
Dworkin, Stephen, 154-55

203

E
Education, importance of, 132-50
Einstein, Albert, 27, 133
Elder, Glen, 93-94, 95
Erikson, Erik, 40, 42, 43
    stages of development, 110, 175

F
Family Circle (magazine), 2, 5, 9, 64
Family stability, importance of, 62-63
Farrell, Suzanne, 4
    mother, 90
Fathers, role of, 4-5, 62-64
Feld, Sheila, 118, 119
Filer, Ehrma, 71, 128, 145, 148-49, 175
Filer, John H., 4
Firstborn children, 21-22
FitzGerald, Frances, 4, 97
Fonda, Jane, 124
Foreman, Carol Tucker, 90
    mother, 116
Freud, Anna, 119
Freud, Sigmund, 10, 40, 64
Fryer, Katherine, 55, 76, 129, 130
Fryer Research Center, The, 129

G
Gardner, Howard, 56, 57
Gardner, John, 9, 14
Gibson, Kenneth, 4, 9-10, 64, 72, 76, 102-3, 117
    mother, 11, 39, 64, 85, 87, 95, 102-3, 130, 158
Gilmore, John, 58-59
Ginzberg, Adele, 129-30
Ginzberg, Eli, 4, 129
Ginzberg, Louis, 129
Goertzel, Mildred, 133
Goertzel, Victor, 133
Gottschalk, Alfred, 4
    mother, 39
Graham, Katherine, 16
Grant Study, The, 119
Growth process, Erikson's stages of, 40-41

Guns of August, The (Tuchman), 29
Guthrie, Marjorie, 50, 88, 104, 130
Guthrie, Woody, 104, 130
Guthrie family, 27

H
Harris, Patricia Roberts, 4
    mother, 133
Harrison, Barbara G., 120
Hennig, Margot, 22, 124
Henson, Jim, 27
Hobbies, 135-36
Holtzman, Elizabeth, 4, 22, 34, 60-61
Holtzman, Filia, 60-61, 88, 130
Homer, Winslow, 55
Hoyer, Linda Grace, 130

I
International Year of the Child, 6

J
Jackson, Irene, 65, 134
Jackson, Mahalia, 126, 127
Jackson, Maynard, 4, 21, 77, 82, 130
Jamison, Judith, 4, 39, 97
Jamison, Tessie, 39, 135
Jordan, Barbara, 29

K
Kaplan, Louise, 42
Keniston, Kenneth, 19
Kirschner, Belle, 39, 69
Kirschner, Don, 69, 85

L
Learning, home as place of, 139-45
Leibowitz, Sarah Fryer, 4, 21, 34, 55, 114, 129, 157
    mother, 37, 90
Levin, Harry, 33
Levinson, Daniel, 126

Index

Lieberman, Joseph, 65, 114-15, 133
Lincoln, Abraham, 37
Little Darlings, The (Cable), 132

M
McBride, Patricia, 4
McClelland, David, 18, 44-45
McCullough, Colleen, 70
MacLaine, Shirley, 92
Maccoby, Eleanor, 33
Mahler, Margaret, 41-42
Making of a Genius, The (Stern), 47
Managerial Woman, The (Hennig), 22
Maslow, Abraham, 11
Maternal involvement, importance of, 38
Matlin, Margaret, 11
May, William F., 4
Meyner, Helen, 34
Mothering, gifted, 30-61 *passim*
Mothers, 11-12, 62-63
  of achievers (by name):
  Bacharach, Burt, 58, 65, 130, 149
  Barksdale, Clarence, 97
  Bell, Larry, 103, 148
  Bloom, Floyd, 97
  Chase, Chevy, 37
  Clarke, John Clem, 93
  Crichton, Michael, 52-53, 63-64, 71, 84, 85, 87, 97, 180
  Dunaway, Faye, 37, 97
  Farrell, Suzanne, 90
  Filer, John H., 71, 128, 145, 148-49, 175
  Foreman, Carol Tucker, 116
  Gibson, Kenneth, 11, 39, 64, 85, 87, 95, 102-3, 130, 158
  Gottschalk, Alfred, 39
  Harris, Patricia, 133
  Holtzman, Elizabeth, 60-61, 88, 130
  Jackson, Maynard, 65, 134
  Jamison, Judith, 39, 135
  Kirschner, Don, 39, 69
  Leibowitz, Sarah, 37, 90
  Moynihan, Daniel P., 133

Mothers *(contd.)*
  Schroeder, Patricia Scott, 95, 109
  Simon, Paul, 38-39
  Tharp, Twyla, 54, 69
  Updike, John, 104, 130, 134
  Warwick, Dionne, 39
  Yalow, Rosalyn, 88, 120
Motivation, 8-9, 14-15
Moynihan, Daniel P., 4, 21
  mother, 133
Mozart, Wolfgang Amadeus, 28

N
Names, importance of, 33
Newell, Barbara, 4, 130
Ney, Edward M., 4
Nuclear radiation, 5-6

O
Oneness and Separateness (Kaplan), 42
Only children, 21-22

P
Parental expectations, effect of, 32-38
Parental interests, 73
Parental neglect, 6-7
"Parental Power by Legitimation and Its Effects on the Adolescent" (Elder), 93-94
Parental roles, 7-8
Parents, 17-18, 173-74
Parent's Monitor and Young People's Friend, The (magazine), 132
Parks, Ross, 64
Parton, Dolly, 21
Patterns of Child Rearing (Sears, Maccoby, and Levin), 33
Patton, George, 133
"Pierre and Friends," 27
Plimpton, George, 4, 21, 90
Pons, Lily, 51
Priceless Gifts (Sugarman), 117
Problem solving, 100-3
Productive Personality, The (Gilmore), 58

Project Zero, 55, 56, 58

R
Reading, 140, 141-42
Rembrandt, 28
Roe, Ann, 133
Role models, 126-31
"Roots of Success, The" (Chance), 2, 7
Rosenthal, Robert, 35

S
St. Laurent, Yves, 26
Sawin, Douglas, 64
Schaefer, Earl, 36
School and parents, partnership of, 145-50
Schrack, Florence, 122
Schroeder, Patricia Scott, 4
  mother, 95, 109
Sears, Robert, 33
Seasons of a Man's Life, The (Levinson), 126
Segal, Julius, 23
Shilling, Clint, 122
Sills, Beverly, 50-51, 52
Silverman, Shirley, 50-51
Simon, Paul, 4, 11
  mother, 38-39
Simon, Sidney, 96
Spitz, René, 49
Stang, David, 11
Stern, Aaron, 47-48
Stern, Edith, 68
Success, signposts for, 171-84
"Successful" children, definition of, 1-2
Sugarman, Daniel, 117
Summer, Donna, 126
Suzuki system, 51-52

T
Taylor, Calvin, 148
Television, dangers of, 136-39
Terman, Lewis, 28
Terman study, 28, 68
Tharp, Twyla, 3-4
  mother, 54, 69
Travolta, John, 28, 120-21
Tree, Marietta, 97, 130, 131, 134
Tuchman, Barbara, 29, 35

U
United Nations, 6
University of California, 119
Updike, John, 4, 66-67, 123, 124
  mother, 104, 130, 134

V
Value rankings, 74-75
Values clarification, 96-100
Violence, television, 6

W
Warwick, Dionne, 3
  mother, 39
Wyeth, Andrew, 65
Wyeth, Caroline, 92
Wyeth, Jamie, 4, 65
Wyeth family, 27

Y
Yalow, Rosalyn, 4, 26, 85, 108, 131, 174
  mother, 88, 120
Young, Andrew, 77, 97

Z
Zajonc, Robert B., 21